A3

Waiting for Dessert

X

Vladimir Estragon

Waiting for Dessert

THE VIKING PRESS   NEW YORK

FOR THE WOMAN WARRIOR, OF COURSE

Library of Congress Cataloging in Publication Data
Estragon, Vladimir, 1940–
  Waiting for dessert.
  1. Gastronomy—Addresses, essays, lectures.
  2. Food—Addresses, essays, lectures.
  3. Cookery—Addresses, essays, lectures. I. Title.
TX631.S83   641'.01'3   81-15929
ISBN 0-670-74864-1   AACR2

Grateful acknowledgment is made to Random House, Inc.,
and Alfredo Viazzi for permission to reprint two recipes
(slightly adapted) from Alfredo Viazzi's Italian Cooking.
Copyright © 1979 by Alfredo Viazzi.

Foreword

*W*e eat, first of all, because we have to, but we also do it for fun, for security, and for love. This book is at least as much about those excitements as it is about food. It could hardly be otherwise, for food—manna from heaven, loaves and fishes, bread and wine—has long been the central public mystery of Western culture. Sex, its only rival, used to be private.

To write about food, then, is to write about how we live *together;* even when dinner conversation was conducted in grunts, efficiency and economy demanded that meals be shared. The logistical pressures may now come more from the way work is organized than from the lack of refrigeration, but most people still feel them as imperatives.

And so this book is very much about families, and about the networks of friendship that we so construct to see us through times, however long, when the traditional family seems undesirable or unattainable on reasonable terms. Tossing such networks into the definitional pot—where as sources of fun, security, and love they belong—I count myself as "pro-family."

In a better world, that would hardly be a ringing declaration, but "family" has become something of a code word, rather the way "crime in the streets" used to be. Pinched, ungenerous spirits are trying to take what belongs to all of us and make it only theirs. They'll fail in the long run—there is too much history going against them—but the immediate American future seems likely to hold an unpleasant dose of "moral" repression. I don't want to sound overearnest—like the meals I cook, these essays are meant for pleasure—but I would hope *Waiting for Dessert* serves as a partial antidote to the poison now threatening the body politic.

The columns that eventually led to this book were first written for *The Village Voice,* and though I'd been fond of the paper long before I began appearing in it, *The Voice* was not among the first places I would have gone to seek a recipe for braised lamb. Offered some nice hash, the average *Voice* reader seemed at least as likely to reach for a small-bowled brass pipe as for a knife and fork. Activities of the former sort can make one mighty hungry indeed, but recipes for satisfying the munchies had better be *very* short and *very* simple. (Something on the line of, "First, open the bag of corn chips; second, eat," would be appropriate.) So when Estragon first tiptoed into the paper, the editors and I regarded it as very much an experiment.

More than four years have passed since that initial appearance, and I'm still at it, but the column itself has gradually changed from the relatively straightforward consideration of various foods to the considerably more difficult question of my relationship to them. I suppose this intrusion of the self is classic "new journalism," but the change occurred less from aesthetics than from necessity. Almost as soon as the column started, my domestic life got ridiculously busy.

When Estragon began, I was divorced and living alone in a small Manhattan apartment. My teen-age children, who had for some time lived around the corner from me, had moved to New Hampshire with their mother, and our only extended time together came during summer vacation, which we spent in a Shelter Island house I shared in quasi-familial fashion with New York neighbors. This settled order was, to my surprise and delight, interrupted by my falling in love with the Woman Warrior. Even more amazing, my feelings were reciprocated, and we began to live together. Almost immediately, it seemed, my older son decided to come down and join us, and "baby" (i.e., the hairy, horny Potato King) made three. A year later, the Mad Baker made a similar trek south.

By then, the economics of Manhattan rents being what they are, we'd moved to Brooklyn, where soon (the economics of Brooklyn rents being what *they* are) we decided to look for a house. With a down payment provided by selling my half of the Shelter Island place to its co-owners, we bought a not-quite crumbling Victorian pile in Flatbush. Somewhere along the way, the Woman Warrior and I married, and soon—nine days too late to qualify for 1979—the Youngest Member arrived, and we had a little tax deduction of our own.

Well! You can imagine how thrilling all this was (to me, at any rate), and these various changes more or less forced their way into the column. For a while, when I first began collecting the pieces for this book, I thought of arranging them chronologically, yielding a sort of domestic novel (or soap opera), but I discovered that I hadn't been quite so obsessed by family as I'd imagined—or at any rate, that the domestic drama hadn't crowded out my other obsessions. I'd spent a lot of time, it developed, poking around in what amounts to epistemology—does food taste good because of itself or because of something in us—and searching in my past—what in it led to a love for food and to the traditionally nonmale role of cook? I'd also found time to notice the world outside—both the changes in seasons that brought new foods to our table and the more dramatic rounds of assassinations, elections, and wars that make up "the news."

And so the book turns out to be organized—to have organized itself, actually—around these recurring concerns. As might have been expected over a four-year period, I occasionally repeated (and sometimes contradicted) myself, and most of the longer essays that follow represent stitched-together and expanded gropings with themes on which I'd played a number of variations.

I owe a great deal to the editors who first saw these pieces into print at *The Voice*—Karen Durbin, M. Mark, and Jan Hoffman—to David Schneiderman, the paper's editor-in-chief, and to Viking's Amanda Vaill, who discerned the book lurking within the heap of columns I dumped on her desk. I am especially grateful to Marianne Partridge, *Voice* editor-in-chief when this enterprise began, not only for nurturing the column through its tentative beginnings, but also for insisting that Estragon have his own name—which she, long before I, knew would eventually lead to his own personality. But my deepest debt, obviously, is to the objective correlatives of the people who appear in this book for allowing me to exaggerate their foibles along with my own; though much of what appears about them—and me—is nearly fiction, I think it's all true.

V.E.

Brooklyn
July 5, 1981

Contents

WHERE THE ANGST IS

PHILOSOFOOD

Portrait of the Artist as a Young Pig

Pictures from Some Institutions

There are a number of pleasant things I remember about Athens, Ohio, a citylet where I did time while studying English during the early sixties. A fine bluegrass band hung around the Sculpture House, the Hocking River flooded spectacularly each spring, and you could buy sweetbreads for nineteen cents a pound at the local Kroger's because nobody wanted 'em. Unfortunately, there was also something called the Gourmet Club, a group of six or eight faculty couples who took turns competitively feeding one another elaborate dinners. Every now and then favored graduate students were invited to one of these funereal feasts, and I suppose I should be grateful, for the joyless tedium of those occasions probably hastened my exit from academia. By me, food is not High Seriousness; it's fun.

The Youngest Member, smarter than most professors, already knows this. If you don't believe it, watch her swoosh the stuff around her mouth, spit it out for inspection, finger-paint with it for a while, then scoop it up to start the process again. You and I no doubt did the same things—certain modes repeat themselves across the most-publicized generation gaps—we just don't remember them anymore.

The first sort of food-as-toy thing I *do* remember—concocting flour and water pastes—was my mother's way to keep her curious toddler occupied and in view while she made dinner. She clonked around over my head; I sat on the floor and mixed a bowl of gloop. It was amusing, and while I'm sure it was hell to clean up, it did keep me out of harm's way. (This had been a subject of considerable concern ever since the night I'd filched a lamb chop from the kitchen counter and run to the bathroom to see if it would fit down the toilet. It did. Since this was a war-time lamb chop, the object of much parental anticipation while the mountain of ration points necessary to acquire it had been saved, I am lucky that roast young Vladimir didn't substitute on the menu.)

But the pleasures of flour and water are not inexhaustible, and as Bo Diddley and St. Paul advise, I eventually put aside the things of childhood (Mr. Diddley, I'm told, fancies fried chicken; Paul dined on grievances) and went on to building sandwiches.

For some reason now thankfully lost in the mists, I used to love lettuce and tomato on mayonnaise-slathered Wonder Bread. (I think it must have been the contrast between the instantly soggy bread and the crisp lettuce; I know I didn't like the bread toasted.) And I made countless peanut-butter-ands. I still eat a few of these combinations (bacon, for instance) but have discarded others. I have a terrible feeling that I might actually like some of them, and perhaps it is false sophistication that prevents me from once again combining peanut butter with Marshmallow Fluff. But perhaps not.

Despite such bits of disgustingness, the sandwich experiments were useful. I learned a lot about textures and developed at least a rudimentary ability to predict whether two flavors would contrast or clash. Taken simply as learning devices, the sandwiches provided—in my case, literally—instant feedback of the sort that school systems are now spending zillions of dollars to achieve through computer installations. Best of all (at least from my parents' point of view), any failures were endured privately, not visited on a table of grimly polite adults.

Since those days my likely sandwich materials have expanded

considerably from the staples available in my parents' *goyische* suburban kitchen; now there's capocolla, lox, prosciutto, alfalfa sprouts, various wursts, and salamis. I even overcome cultural prejudice and make odd California combinations, like the Monterey. But all these pale compared to the memory of a sandwich I almost never made at home.

For years, in fact, I thought it was called a club sandwich because the Larchmont Yacht Club was where you got it. It was special, not only because of its ingredients (how often, after all, was there leftover turkey around the house?), but because it was a sort of forbidden thrill, like hamburgers on Friday (because, honest, I'd already ordered before I remembered what day it was, and it's a worse sin to waste food than to eat meat on Fridays).

For seven summers, from the time I was old enough to go sailing alone until I turned fifteen and started summer jobs, those good, greasy snack-bar hamburgers were a four-day-a-week staple. But sometimes—ah, sometimes—either family disorganization or my own stupidity would see me at the club with no lunch money. On those days I would go upstairs to the screened-off section of the dining room where one didn't need a coat and tie, and I would charge my lunch.

Always it was a club sandwich, the toast brown and crisp, the turkey moist with mayonnaise, the bacon sharp and smoky. The sandwich sat in the center of the plate, each of its triangular quarters secured by a toothpick. Next to it, on a single leaf of Boston lettuce, were two small gherkins. I ate those first, getting them out of the way before starting on the milk. And then, either in solitary glory or with the kids whose families let them eat upstairs every day, I looked out over the boats rocking at their moorings and lazily worked my way through each triangle. The waiter called me "sir," the tablecloth was white—and I was very fond of sandwiches.

We were eventually bounced from the Yacht Club when my father, jobless, could no longer pay the bills. He died a few years later, missing my various marriages and children, and I've often wondered what he would make of them—and of me. But he is frozen in time, and I'm never older than seventeen, confused and missing him.

He might, of course, have disapproved. I've heard my mother proudly telling people, "Vladimir used to be such a cute little boy," but she always seems miffed that this middle-aged man has usurped that nice boy's place. I understand how she feels; even when the Potato King comes downstairs fresh from his morning shave, I can still see traces of the five-year-old's milk mustache at the corners of his mouth. I suppose it will always be there.

But except for those painful moments when they smash head-on, runaway trains spewing bodies and suitcases through the night, such reciprocal memories hold parents and children together. By now, for instance, I don't remember where the trip began, only that it ended at Grand Central. My mother and father sat in the carriage; I—seven years old, perhaps, and wriggling with excitement—was up front. As we rode down Fifth Avenue, the hansom driver let me take the reins. Not for long, I suppose, but long enough that the moment remains with me after more than three decades.

Five or six years later I was in the hospital. I'd mistakenly attempted to field a foul tip with my left eye and had been sent to the New York Eye and Ear Infirmary for tests and a possible operation. It was a long way from home, in some then exotic corner of Manhattan, but my parents visited me regularly. One night they arrived with a sandwich. Thick slices of roast pork, lettuce and tomato, white bread. The meat was salty, its firm fibrous texture blissfully unlike hospital food. I can still, in my mind's mouth, taste that sandwich whenever I want.

Why, I wonder now, *that* sandwich? Why the pull of the horse as it clopped down Fifth Avenue? There are nickel psychological explanations—the discovery of autonomy, the reaffirmation of parental love—but I don't quite believe them. They are too comforting. Yes, I wanted to break free of my parents, and of course I wanted to be hugged and forgiven after I'd hurt myself (still do, I suppose), but any kid's growing up is a parade of proto-autonomy and recaptured infancy. What singles out these marchers?

The ride in the hansom cab was *supposed* to be special, a once-in-a-lifetime treat. The sandwich was, well, a sandwich, yet the memory of it is there not just when I choose to call it up, but is continually present as an ideal, informing all other sandwiches.

This random quality of memory at once disturbs and delights me. My parents—I know because I've asked—had no notion they were doing anything extraordinary when they brought me the sandwich. It was from some luncheonette that had nothing to recommend it except a location near the hospital, and I had to prompt my mother for her to remember even that much. She seemed, indeed, mystified by the question.

But selective memory is more than odd; it's scary. What do (or will, in the case of the Youngest Member) *my* kids remember? What of me will they carry with them? The horse and the sandwich imply that virtually *anything* can turn out to be important, that some offhand remark or gesture I've already forgotten may reappear in my kids' lives long after my conscious pedagogy has faded into the wallpaper. If even the most casual interchange can become an emotional supertanker, there's no such thing as parent's day off.

But precisely because it is inescapable, the burden is liberating. If one can't ever tell what will stick in a kid's mind, my most horrific screw-ups may not matter—or have mattered—at all.

The "or have mattered" is there because the Potato King, my child always, has become his own man. Time and an airplane have taken him off to college, and he will never again live here in quite the way he did even last week. Carrying two duffel bags and a typewriter in his hands, and God knows what in his head, he is gone. He has left behind a new address, an unfamiliar area code, and a damp towel on the bathroom floor.

Also, some memories of his own. The night before leaving he took us out to dinner. We sat, a family of five, in the Elm Room at Tavern on the Green (a swell place to bring an infant, it turns out) and did our best not to talk about departing flights. The Youngest Member, decked out in a sailor suit and proudly enthroned on a booster chair, ate her first strawberry. I had calf's liver, and one horrible future-lurch when I imagined her going as well. Then, I thought, like the English middle classes, I shall go to the sea and die.

But when we got outside the Potato King had a hansom waiting to take us to the subway, and we went home to Brooklyn instead.

Little Leek,
Who Made Thee?

*D*r. Pressclips dropped by the office the other day to smoke a cigarette (of mine) and talk about a menu (of his). It involved something he described as "baby lamb in hay." I have been in the good doctor's apartment, and though it has many sterling qualities, a large open pit is not among them. (Neither was a bale of hay, for that matter, but the omission might have been seasonal.) Ignoring, for the moment, the question of hay, I asked where he planned to cook the beast. In the oven, he said.

Dear God, has the man no shame? Is he truly willing to twist a little lambie into horribly contorted positions so that he can jam it into the oven for the pleasure of his friends? Shocked, I was. Dismayed. Yet he seemed almost preternaturally calm and was no doubt ready to burble on about the mysterious hay, when I managed to ask just how he planned to arrange the carcass during cooking.

Well, lo and behold, dear readers, it turns out that what the esteemed pundit had in mind was a *leg* of lamb—a prospect perhaps discomfiting to vegetarians but considerably less macabre than I had imagined. Mutually relieved by the evaporation of the slight cloud of distrust that had momentarily impaired our usually perfect harmony (if only the Irish could learn to mention parts of the body in public), we agreed that all this talk of dinner had made us hungry, so it was off to Café Loup. There, over a splendid lunch (he: mussel soup and smoked trout; I: grilled sole), we glided quickly over the oil crisis and various other frivolities, settling down eventually to a serious discussion of memorable meals.

Pressclips, something of a gadabout, waxed obsessive over a particular dish of mushrooms and truffles he'd had in Venice, leading me to lament the decline of Luchow's and its once-glorious platters of sautéed Black Forest mushrooms. The pleasures of Luchow's having departed this country long before Dr. P.'s arrival here, he found even the notion of a decent Luchow's unbelievable, though he admitted to eating there occasionally. We decided—since one eats among lederhosen only when one has forgotten how wretched one's previous meal there was—that the interval between Luchow lunches was a functional test of memory span. After that we had some more wine.

I then mentioned that the nice folks at Random House had sent me a copy of *Alfredo Viazzi's Italian Cooking,* which news started a veritable flood of reminiscences about Sr. Viazzi's Bank Street trattoria. At one point, pushed to the wall by the doctor's ruthless probing, I admitted that I'd probably had more good meals there than at any other restaurant in the world. And, more to the point, that I'd ripped off more ideas from Viazzi than I cared to confess.

Notwithstanding all that, the new cookbook came as a revelation, for its relentlessly unclassical idiosyncrasies gave me the feeling that I was actually standing in the kitchen with Viazzi, sharing with him the process of creation. The 150 or so recipes are crammed with pinches of this and little bits of that, so much so that they read as though the spices would all cancel each other out in some gunky sort of sludge. Not so. I've now done about a half dozen meals from the book—some new to me, some I'd previously attempted—and they have been unfailingly delicious.

Indeed, so lurid was my description of a leek-and-pasta dish that Dr. P. was moved to abandon his plans for lamb and prepare the Viazzi creation instead. Probably just as well. I understand now about the lamb, but the notion of an ovenful of hay seems risky to me.

~~~~~~~~~~

TAGLIARINI VERDI AL GUANCIALE
(*adapted from* Alfredo Viazzi's Italian Cooking)

1. Cut two bunches of leeks, white parts only, into julienne strips (being especially careful to turn the fibrous core, if any, into matchstick-size pieces). Rinse, dry and slowly sauté in 2 tablespoons of butter along with six whole peppercorns, a tablespoon of chopped fresh Italian parsley, a pinch of nutmeg, and a dusting of salt.

2. Chop a third of a pound of pancetta (Italian bacon) into quarter-inch cubes and sauté in a separate pan until crisp. Drain onto paper towels and reserve.

3. As soon as the leeks have softened and become translucent, set them aside and cook one pound of green tagliarini (narrow-cut pasta) until just barely done. Drain the pasta into a colander, put the pan back on the fire, and melt a half-stick of butter in it.

4. Reduce heat slightly, return the pasta to the pan, and mix with the melted butter. After about a minute add the leek mixture and the pancetta, and continue stirring. Add 1 cup of heavy cream and ¼ cup grated Parmesan, and continue stirring until the sauce is thoroughly hot and coats the pasta (about two minutes). Serve with extra cheese.

5. Buy Viazzi's book.

The Hot Dogs of Summer

*T*he song is from a car commercial. To an infuriatingly memorable tune, teeming hordes of racially balanced Norman Rockwell Americans dance about their daily business, singing of hot dogs, baseball, and apple pie. After that, an announcer ladles on a few phrases about America coming home to Chevrolet. All of which, though the frankfurter is not named after the small city in Kentucky, is presumably supposed to make us eschew the Volkswagen.

Mostly, it makes me hungry. (Psychiatrist to patient: "But why does the Empire State Building remind you of sex?" Patient, helplessly: "*Everything* does.") For hot dogs.

Though regarded with disdain by the chic, and horror by the alfalfa-sprout crowd, hot dogs are flat-out wonderful. And versatile. Dripping with hot onions and ball-park mustard from a Sabrett man, they taste like New York; served in little cardboard doo-hickeys and called grilled frankforts, they taste like America. They also make no unreasonable demands on the home cook.

Sometimes, however, home cooks make unreasonable demands on them. There are basically three ways to serve hot dogs—boiled, grilled, and disguised. The last way is a mistake. No matter what it says on the covers of those magazines at the supermarket checkout counter, there simply are not 87 Penny-Savings Ways to Thrill Your Family with Frankfurters. The only thing at all thrilling about hot dogs is how street vendors acquire their corners, a question well beyond the concerns of the home cook unless he or she also happens to have subpoena powers. Hot dogs do not thrill; they *remind.*

Which is why I am awestruck by the commercial genius of the Colonial Beef Frank Co., Inc. These wily New England merchants, purveyors of a genuinely undistinguished product, have come up with the brilliant notion of naming their hot dogs after baseball teams—their slogan: "The taste that takes you out to the ball park."

Look out, Proust. Here come truckloads of hot dogs—indistinguishable but for their names—carrying the weight of a thousand April hopes and August disappointments. Or the other way round, for the ball park in one's mind is an unalterably private place. One may be aware, of course, of other fans spread out along the mental grandstands, but the diamond is one's own. On it Joe DiMaggio effortlessly chases down impossible fly balls, and Lou Piniella swings the prettiest bat in baseball. Or maybe Ted Williams disdains, again, the sure hit to the opposite field, and Dwight Evans flings a long strike to cut down an enemy runner at third.

In the very richness of these reveries, however, there is a core of danger that the Colonial folks have conveniently ignored. Viz., what happens when there is a house divided against itself? How can I, with more than thirty summers of love offered to the Red Sox, taste anything but sawdust in a Yankee Frank? And to my oldest, a Yankee interloper in Red Sox territory, Fenway Franks must be bitter fruit. Indeed, to his chagrin, he mistakenly purchased some the other day and swore that they were inferior in every way to those packaged in a different wrapper.

Listen, Colonial, you're playing with fire here. Good cooks have always known that the presentation of a meal (candlelight, flowers, a skillful balance of colors and textures on the plate) changes the way it tastes, but you go too far. To sell a few extra hot dogs, you would drive families asunder. Which is, I suppose, at least as American as General Motors.

Batter Is Thicker than Water

I made a great heap of doughnuts the other morning (a few—real good if you pop 'em into a 400-degree oven for a couple of minutes—are still in the freezer), and as often happens, a taste came wrapped in memories; with the first bite I found myself thinking about my grandmother. My father's mother, that is. She lived with my parents from the time I was about eight or nine, and she made wonderful doughnuts. Helluva fine *crème brûlée*, too.

My maternal grandmother, a woman who often thought she was being principled when she was merely being unpleasant, made only trouble. She also turned off her hearing aid during arguments. She and her older sister—in every respect her polar opposite—arrived at our house a few years after my father's mother, and the three ladies remained with us until their deaths some dozen years later.

All in all, I found the arrangement a favorable one; when my mother was too busy to give me the attention I was convinced I deserved, I could always find someone to be my audience. Mostly this meant I got told how clever I was, but my maternal grandmother was always good for a fight.

She collected affronts as avidly as I collected baseball cards: A luncheon serving of beef liver instead of calf's was good for a week of muttering, and of course any unkindness to Senator Joseph McCarthy was treason pure and simple. Once a Democrat, my grandmother had mourned abed for three days after Al Smith's 1928 defeat; she rose a rock-ribbed Republican with a keen hearing aid for Commies and their liberal dupes (my father, for instance, and eventually me).

About housework, however, my grandmother's attitude remained fixed. It was beneath her. That was why decent families had servants. We were, by that definition, indecent, so when my great-aunt pitched in and helped out, she was—like that horrid Roosevelt—a traitor to her class. I think that's really why my grandmother kicked her into the radiator.

She said she did it because my aunt was blocking her path to the bathroom, but I think she was infuriated simply by seeing her sister on her hands and knees, wiping up some spilled tea. And so, bracing herself with her canes, she took aim at my aunt's ample rump and planted one. My aunt lurched forward, banged her head against the radiator, and fell, semiconscious and bleeding, to the floor, where despite her sister's repeated instructions to get up, she lay.

After a while even my grandmother began to think she might have gone too far, and she stumped off to call the doctor. This operation was rendered difficult, however, for she was so nervous that she kept forgetting to move the receiver down to her breast so she could hear the doctor's end of the conversation. He, figuring that my mother wasn't home and that *something* had gone wrong, decided to send an ambulance.

It, the neighbors, and my mother arrived in rapid-fire order, and my aunt—still bleeding spectacularly but not seriously injured—was whisked off to the hospital for a couple of stitches. She was back in an hour and was resting on the living room couch, her forehead a great lump of bandages, when my father's mother came home from work.

"Good lord, Min!" she said. "Whatever happened to you?"

My aunt, ever ready to put the best face on things, sipped her tea and replied, "I was cleaning the kitchen floor, and I fell."

The freshly arrived grandmother began offering sympathy but was forestalled by the victim's sister. Whirring furiously back and forth in the low rocker, she interrupted. "Did not!" she snapped. "The old fool was in my way, so I pushed her." Then she went to bed.

By the next morning, the incident was on its way to becoming family folklore, and since there'd been no harm done, it was a pleasure to have the memory along with my doughnuts. The ease with which near-tragedy was converted to domestic comedy was typical of my parents' household, and it may be that the ability to find humor in out-of-the-way situations is a hallmark of successful families. But to the spontaneous cushioning of unpleasantness that is a reasonable enough defensive reflex, my family added a layer of propriety from the three aging ladies. This was more shabby-genteel than spontaneous.

For example, though my paternal grandmother was something of a specialist at producing mysterious casseroles, she would never allow the term "leftovers" to sully her lips; instead, they were rallagazooks. Standard usage was "ham rallagazooks," but when she was feeling fancy-schmancy, we ate "rallagazooks of ham." I'm not sure that leftovers tasted any better (or worse) in their gussied-up nomenclature, but my grandmother was a firm believer in the notion that a rose would damn well not smell so sweet if everyone called it a liverwort.

Fair enough, for she was something of an expert on the value of names. She became a domestic after her husband died, but of a rank at which her employers' children were expected to address her as "Mrs. E." She would not, I think, have taken a job where they addressed her as Mary; first names were for maids and handymen. Though she is long dead, I figured out only recently that her coinage for leftovers hadn't been part of her experience as a mother but a device to inveigle the children of the wealthy into eating their hash.

I discovered this when the kids gave the Woman Warrior a present. I'm not sure what the proper department-store name for the item is—bed rest, maybe?—but it was one of those bulky pillows-with-arms that you lean up against the headboard for sitting up in bed and reading. It was a wonderful present, and both the Woman Warrior and I applauded it. But in the midst of our babble of praise, we suddenly stopped and looked at each other funny; she had called the gift "a husband," while I'd identified it as "Penelope." That's what we'd called them when we were growing up and sometimes got to use one when we were sick and had to stay home in bed all day.

Both of us, it turned out, meant the same thing: something so dependable that you could lean on it whenever you wanted. My family had been driven back to the Greeks for an appropriate symbol; hers, more optimistic, had chosen ahistoric marriage.

I still call it Penelope. This is not stubbornness or even ideology (though I do find a pillow a somewhat passive role model), but habit. The names we use for things as kids stick; in your secret heart, what do you call your sexual parts?

Anyway, though I sometimes hear myself saying "rallagazooks," my father never used the word. Which is why I suspect—though there is no way of confirming it, for he died even before my grandmother—that it wasn't part of his upbringing. As far as I remember, he had only one family coinage for leftovers, and that was of a fairly specialized sort. He called the dregs of yesterday's coffee, which he would heat up and drink while making the morning's fresh pot, "the Phidipedes," a nod to the original marathoner, apparently referring to the coffee's staying power.

Oddly, it's not a term I use, though I would recognize it instantly. But I still sometimes refer to dirty pots and pans as "the don't-counts." This usage derives from my parents' habit (which I found strange at the time, and my own kids would surely view as evidence of derangement) of doing dishes even when it wasn't their turn. On one such occasion, when my mother was slated for scullery work, she heard my father running an awful lot of water for someone who was in the kitchen only to get the after-dinner coffee. "Are you doing the dishes?" she called.

"No," he said. But the water continued to run, and there was a great clanging and banging of metal.

"Well, what *are* you doing?"

Silence, except of course for the noise of someone obviously washing dishes. And then, the water off, my father appearing at the door, proudly wiping his hands on a dish towel. "I *was* doing the pots and pans," he said, "and they don't count."

I miss him. I even miss the three ladies in their infinite variety. They are with me, however, not only in doughnuts but in words. For as I always say, one nice thing about rallagazooks is you don't have a whole lot of don't-counts to do.

FRESH-AND-DRIED PEA SOUP

This is not my family's version but the Woman Warrior's own distillation from a half dozen recipes. Delicious on its own, it is spiced with the knowledge that it is the last rallagazook from another monster ham.

1. To 5 qts. of liquid (chicken stock and water in about a 3-to-2 ratio, with a little white wine if there's none already in the stock) in a heavy pot, add 2 heaping cups of dried split green peas and the hambone (still bearing the bits of ham that haven't become sandwiches, ham-and-macaroni-and-cheese, eggs Benedict, etc.). Bring the water to a boil, skim, reduce heat, and simmer, covered, for about an hour.

2. While the peas are cooking, chop 1 medium onion and 1 good-sized carrot into as small a dice as your patience allows. Sauté them, slowly, in a couple of tablespoons butter. After they've softened, add the chopped green parts of a large leek and 2 generous handfuls shredded lettuce (romaine is nice, Boston

too) to the pan and continue cooking for another 5 or 10 minutes.

3. When the split peas have pretty much dissolved, remove the hambone from the pot and pick from it any chunks of meat that haven't already fallen off. Shred them, if necessary, and return them to the pot along with sautéed vegetables, a large bay leaf, 1 teaspoon sugar, a good sprinkle of white pepper and dried thyme, and 1 cup fresh peas (or ½ package frozen). Add more liquid if required and continue simmering for about 20 minutes.

4. Just before serving—ideally with a good crusty French bread—stir in heavy cream to taste. A half cup is probably all right, but more will do no harm. Serves 4 to 6.

If eggs Benedict, the last pre-soup gasp of ham, rank high on the scale of luxurious leftovers, one would think that hash is somewhat near the bottom. Not so. Hash has indeed suffered grievously at the hands of the canning industry, but it isn't necessarily susceptible to Gresham's Law (as anyone who's tasted the Algonquin's elegant chicken hash will be pleased to testify).

Nevertheless, the dish has been so discredited that if the boss tells you you've made a hash of something, you would be prudent not to regard this as a compliment. Arriving safely home, however, you can set to work with a knife and ease your pains with a dinner that will provide ironic as well as gustatory pleasure.

ROAST BEEF HASH

1. Dice 2 medium onions and cook them slowly in a couple of tablespoons butter in a heavy covered skillet.

2. When the onions are soft, add 2 or 3 cups chopped cooked potatoes (ideally they should have been roasted with the meat, but newly boiled will do). Increase the heat to moderate, and stir occasionally. If the potatoes start to stick, add more butter.

3. Chop (*hacher*, French, to cut) 4 thick slices *rare* roast beef

in small pieces and add to the pan. If the beef was adequately seasoned before roasting, you need add only salt, pepper, and a bunch of chopped parsley; if it seemed a little bland, thyme and minced garlic would be in order.

4. Press the stirred ingredients together into a more-or-less cake and increase the heat again. As soon as the bottom gets crusty, flip the cake (in sections, if necessary) and lower the heat. When the hash is warmed through, it's ready to eat.

P.S. My mother read this recipe after it was first published; she suggests a little heavy cream "for binding."

Strings Attached

Chestnuts are beautiful. I was first captivated by them in grammar school, when autumn brought a year's worth of horse chestnuts to the ground. Gathering them was boy-sport, and we would bring home the largest we could find, pierce them with a needle, and thread each one at the end of a knotted string. We oiled them as well, rubbed them till they glowed, chose favorites . . . and then we put them at risk.

The game was called "threesies." One player let his prize chestnut hang, describing gentle circles in the breeze; a rival warrior, taking a firm grip on his own champion, was allowed to swing it three times at the pendant victim. If neither nut was shattered, the players exchanged roles for another round. The game continued until one chestnut or another tumbled in pieces to the ground.

We learned, I suppose, hand-eye coordination that way—it is not the easiest thing in the world to control the arc of a killer chestnut—but something about the nature of loss as well. You could always win back a favorite marble; the chestnut was gone.

On the other hand, chestnuts were abundant in their season. Free for the gathering, they were "worth" only what one had invested in them emotionally. Triumph—the simple fact of winning—probably would have felt the same whether we had polished our chestnuts or not, but losing was different. That hurt us more because we had dared to inform these found objects with meaning, and played, finally, against ourselves. So to make a particular chestnut too much one's favorite was almost to guarantee its destruction. One became cautious with it, and it was smashed by some freckle-faced innocent who thought all chestnuts were the same. They weren't, they aren't, and John Lennon will never sing again.

I heard the news about four hours ago. The phone rang, someone told me, and I haven't been able to sleep. I thought the typewriter might be an escape, but it hasn't worked out that way. I'd been planning to write about chestnuts since Thanksgiving, and as the clock chimed three and I rolled from side to side, they seemed an eminently safe retreat.

I should have known better; they've let me down before. I ate chestnuts in Paris once, three years after the Beatles had broken up, because it seemed a romantic thing to do. We bought them from a street vendor, then sat in some nameless square, peeling them and practicing our French. They weren't very good, and neither was I. I was peeling chestnuts, walking the cobbled streets around Contrescarpe, and slowly discovering that I wasn't at all in love with my companion. But here we were in Paris, spending our hard-earned pounds on a brief holiday, and I was determined not to spoil it for her—or maybe I just didn't want to spoil the gauzy lovers' Paris I'd always wanted to be part of. I did, of course, but the strain of trying not to turned the chestnuts bitter in my mouth. It was six years before I went back to Paris, and it wasn't until last Thanksgiving that I ate another chestnut. Both were better this time round.

"I really thought love would save us all." John said that once. I don't know. But it is dawn now, and a distant bird—unconscious of its irony—is singing, and I want to believe him. So I'm remembering that love changes chestnuts, which is not a bad thing to say about either of them. Still, a force that powerful is dangerous. It was, after all, a fan who waited in the shadows for John.

~~~~~~~~

BRUSSELS SPROUTS WITH CHESTNUTS

When we went to the fruit stand to do our Thanksgiving shopping, we discovered that the year had seen its last lima beans. But we did find huge stalks of Brussels sprouts, which went just fine with the chestnuts left over from the turkey stuffing.

1. Simmer 1 cup of peeled chestnuts in chicken stock for about 10 or 15 minutes. Skim them out and add 1 lb. sprouts to the pot. Cook them until just barely tender and drain.

2. In a heavy frying pan melt 3 tablespoons butter with 2 teaspoons brown sugar. Add chestnuts and sprouts, and stir until they are totally coated. (The chestnuts should break up into small pieces.) Lower the heat. Cover the pan and cook them, shaking occasionally until the chestnuts have crisped—about 5 minutes.

Cultured
Gentleman, 38...

What with schisms and isms and endorphins and radioactive iodine to keep up with, the average full-time dilettante has an increasingly difficult row to hoe. One has barely polished off the musings of a botanist from Leeds in the latest *New York Review* when the mailman is hammering at the door with *The New Yorker*, *The Nation*, and *The Old-House Journal*. And as though the information explosion alone isn't trouble enough, magazine publishers have further complicated my life by adding sections of classifieds.

I can't resist their subtle blandishments; the endless rivers of agate type have but to beckon and I am in their thrall. (I don't actually believe that Mary Gordon is seeking companions through an *NYR* "Personal," for instance, but I have to check it out. And who's to tell when I'll need the Levelor Rivieras—whatever they are—that are always advertised in *New York* mag.) On bad days, when the D train takes one of its unscheduled siestas on the Manhattan Bridge, I can even amuse myself with newspaper classifieds.

None of this would really be bad, mind you, except that I find myself *remembering* classified ads. INTERESTING MAILS EVERY DAY, for one. It used to run every month in *Popular Science* and in *Mechanix Illustrated*, and though I haven't read those journals in more than twenty years, it danced across my brain pan shortly after I'd slogged through today's mail. Not the stuff we got at home—which was the usual mix of magazines and veiled threats from creditors—but the heap awaiting me in the office. "Interesting," it no doubt is, in much the same way that an unanticipated visit from Jo-Jo the Dog-Faced Boy might be, but much of it seems to have made its way to me by processes too bizarre to fathom. (Note to Phoenix Gallery: I am not now, nor have I ever been, the Arts Editor of *The Village Voice*. But I think your postcards are real pretty.)

Some of it is right on target, though. Even now, there is on my desk an invitation to "a Bacchanalian festival of chocolate and champagne," which piques the old interest considerably more than, say, news that the New York City Rehabilitation Mortgage Insurance Corporation will be meeting at 2:30 p.m. on May 14. There is also a new paperback called *The Food Lover's Book of Lists*, a confection so on-target as to be positively embarrassing.

This newly arrived volume is, as you might intuit from its title, very much a nonbook, but I forgive it. Where else, for instance, could I learn that 66 of America's 88 pretzel factories are located in Pennsylvania? Or that King John of England expired after dining on lamprey eels?

Not that this stuff is important, mind you, but it plays nicely to my passions for print and for food. Nevertheless, even I was a little stunned by a chart measuring the relative frequency of letters in Campbell's Alphabet Soup. Sure, it's nice to know that there are 14 H's for every 2 K's—a factoid that will clog up my brain for some time, I fear—but it's not as interesting as imagining the research that went into the chart. Did the authors race home from their jobs at *The Washington Star* to paw through countless cans of strained soup? Were they absolutely sure their eighth P wasn't actually a broken R? And how many cans did they use to achieve statistical reliability? One has only to imagine their splendid obsessiveness to be chastened.

To be horrified, however, one has only to imagine them calling Campbell's and asking some poor flack to come up with the figures for them. Not because there is anything dishonest in such researches—nowhere do they claim to have hand-counted the slippery little characters—but because one knows deep down that, like every other food-processing company, Campbell's employs someone whose job it is to answer such questions. And to send me Interesting Mails Every Day.

The Fantastic Four

Beauty Is Food, Food Beauty

I've never approved of the notion that summer and winter cooking should be radically different. The ingredients will vary with the seasons, of course (what churl would pass up summer's confluence of pungent fresh basil and real tomatoes?), but you would not see me turning my nose up at roast beef and Yorkshire pudding in July or a garlicky Caesar salad in January. If it's good at all, it's good anytime.

I understand the idea that at a certain temperature the ideal dinner is a large block of ice, but I've never been impelled to follow it. My approach, though reflected neither in my genes nor in my politics, is fundamentally Anglo-Indian. Fight fire with fire, and pass the beer, please.

Last week's heat wave, however, put this bias to the test. When it gets to 101 degrees, it's no longer merely summer; it's off the chart. Sort of like there are short people, tall people, and then there's Kareem. So when I proposed a chicken paprikash for Friday dinner and the Woman Warrior protested that the dish was too hot, I didn't fight her. I made a meatball stroganoff instead (which she thought was every bit as out-of-season, but we had to use the leftover sour cream somehow, right?).

We did, I admit, dine on chocolate milkshakes last Saturday, but I'm not sure that counts. True, milkshakes approach the minimalists' ice block, but we weren't really hungry. We'd been at the track all day, drinking beer and eating hot dogs (as well as some fried chicken that would have been rejected at the meanest cuchifrito joint on Avenue B). If anything, the milkshakes were extra, a Flatbush champagne to celebrate the timely arrival of a 17-to-1 shot in the sixth race.

Sunday was more of a traditional summer feed, but that was because we fucked up. Since I was scheduled to play in a tennis tournament, I figured the Woman Warrior would handle the food shopping; since she had a complicated interview to do, she thought I would. Result: no shopping. Further result: harsh words. Gone, gone, all too soon gone, the joy of watching a long shot galloping home with its number printed on the ticket in your pocket. In its place, slamming doors, ill will, and high humidity. Followed, fortunately, by the realization that we were suffering from emotional heat rash. Final fade: apologies, hugs and kisses, continuing hunger. "Love in a hut, with water and a crust,/Is—Love, forgive us—cinders, ashes, dust." Which is to say the dinner problem remained.

So anyway, Sunday dinner involved a certain amount of rooting around in the refrigerator and eventually took the form of a cold pasta salad. This seemed eminently in keeping with the season but gave rise to still further philosophical debate: viz., can a meal that is served cold but requires a lot of cooking be legitimately counted as summer food? This seems to me an altogether trickier question than those involving only the finished product, for if one takes the amount of heat generated in the kitchen as the distinction between summer and winter cooking, I can see merit in the argument. The end result may be substantially the same to the consumer—swordfish grilled outdoors over charcoal vs. swordfish broiled in a stove, for example—but makes God's plenty of difference to the cook. Thus *oeuf en gelée,* a classically perfect summer dish from the diner's point of view, is too much of a hassle from the cook's.

But appealing as this logic is, it's fraught with political problems. Also utilitarian ones. Trying to apply the felicific calculus to the *oeuf en gelée* problem, for example, leads one to unanswerable questions about how many diners—all presumed to enjoy *oeufs en gelée* to some as yet unquantified degree—are required to offset the suffering of the cook. Inevitable result: harsh words and slamming doors. Better you should forget the notion of summer food entirely. If you can't stand the heat, go out to dinner.

Which is what we did the next night. Couscous. Perfect summer food.

PASTA LAMIA

1. Chop into pieces roughly the size of your pinky nail: 2 large ripe tomatoes, a medium red onion, and ¼ cup fresh basil leaves. Mix these together thoroughly in a serving bowl with a few tablespoons olive oil and a sprinkling of red wine vinegar and set aside.

2. Prepare, in the usual manner, 1 lb. thin spaghetti. While you are waiting around for the water to boil, cook ½ lb. sliced bacon until crisp. Drain it on paper towels, and as soon as it's cool enough to handle, crumble and add the bits to the tomato and onion mixture.

3. Pour off all but about 2 tablespoons bacon fat, reheat the pan to high, and quickly sauté 1 very large (or 2 small) boneless chicken breast(s) cut in pieces the same size as the tomatoes. Remove from the pan, drain, let cool, and add to the other ingredients.

4. When the pasta is just cooked, drain it in a colander and douse it liberally with cold water, stirring as you do so. When it's cold, add it to the serving bowl. Mix the whole mess together with ½ cup mayonnaise (or more, to taste), give it several firm grates of the pepper mill, and serve. (Note: a good grade of commercial mayonnaise is perfectly okay for this dish; a homemade blend—using a 3-to-1 ratio of vegetable to olive oils—is better.)

Everything in the Garden

The Reverend W. A. Spooner (an otherwise unremarkable Victorian clergyman who once urged his congregation to join him in singing "Let Kinkering Kongs Their Tatles Tyke") bequeathed us the Spoonerism, but it was my mother who turned the form into high domestic art. Her essays in the Spooner mode were always decorative, but, when they occurred in the heat of household battle, often functional as well; nothing ended an escalating argument quite so thoroughly as the mutual giggling fit following a passionate, "Vladinow, stop that right *mir!!*"

She was also a skilled practitioner of the threat-too-awful-to-be-named ("Come down out of that tree or I'll . . . I'll . . . I'll . . ."), a technique that, as the realization of the trap she'd dug for herself spread across her face, similarly produced the giggle effect. Since it also produced me from the tree, confident that I'd receive nothing more dramatic than a hug, there may have been considerable method in her malaprop, but my own experiences with children and trees leads me to believe that no parent is quite *that* clever.

Yet among the catalog of Ma Estragon's Own Elephant Pits that she now redigs to the delight of her grandchildren, her favorite falls into neither of the above categories; instead, she relishes a brilliant example of the Portentous Meaningless that occurred one afternoon when she was telephoning a PTA crony. They were juggling committee schedules around the Thanksgiving vacation, and with the radio generation's usual aversion to dead air, she vamped while organizing her thoughts. She had gotten only as far as, "Let's see, November comes in on the first this year," before she dissolved into whoops of helpless laughter.

My mother could no doubt have kept this particular gem from the family canon by maintaining a decent silence about that conversation, but she was unable to resist sharing it— whoops and all. Thus it was her generosity that enabled me to greet the opening sentence of the agricultural column in a recent *Shelter Island Reporter* like a favorite grade-school friend I'd heard about, but not seen, for thirty years. "Due to a wet May and early June," it began (whoop! whoop!), "the local strawberry crop has been short and should be about over when this is read."

Now, nice as it was to be reminded of my mother's gaffe, the second part of that sentence is a killer. What the opening phrase giveth in the way of amusement, the independent clause vigorously snatcheth away. No strawberries. Thinking about that for a minute, I realized I'd rather see a basket of ripe, just-picked strawberries than a whole busload of my wrinkling classmates from the Chatsworth Avenue School. I never met a strawberry I didn't like.

(Was it Lamb who suggested that Izaak Walton was "a strawberry among men, natural and perfect," and Dr. Johnson who topped him: "The fault in that comparison, sir, is that one cannot tell whether the compliment is greater to the man or to the fruit"? Probably not, Lamb was only nine when Johnson died. Maybe I made the whole thing up.)

Anyway, there are no strawberries and no Dr. Johnsons here; there is only the *Reporter*'s agricultural Cassandra and his further bad news: "Sweet corn, melons, and tomatoes, which are subtropical crops and need heat, are advancing slowly due to the cool nights and days."

"Advancing slowly" isn't the half of it. By this time of year, when the Independence Day oratory has finally died away, Shelter Island is usually awash in tomatoes (and by mid-August, it's dangerous to leave your house unguarded for fear some desperate neighborhood gardener will sneak in and leave a bag of them on your kitchen table). But no. Instead of glut we have shortage. Even George Blados's superdependable farmstand has run dry. On Saturday it displayed a sign reading NO TOMATOES. On Sunday it had been amended to include the word SORRY. And on Monday a further addition read MAYBE WEDNESDAY. Even with this summer's odd-even rationing, it's easier to get gasoline than tomatoes, and gas isn't nearly as tasty.

Still, nature is infinitely kinder than the oil cartel, and if the cool, wet spring delayed the corn and tomatoes, it prolonged the bearing life of the pea crop. Let's hear it for fresh pea soup!

You may notice that the cheerleading for fresh pea soup seems a little, well, forced. You're right. It is a favorite dish, but even it can't quite make up for nature's unpredictability. Maybe if my country life consisted of something more than stolen snatches of summer, I could face aberrant weather with equanimity, but I'm fundamentally a city kid and still have a textbook notion of how seasons are supposed to behave.

That's not to say that New York City weather is unimportant. Nosirree. I take it as a given that New York is more interesting than Los Angeles (I mean, the Eagles and the Dodgers vs. the Talking Heads and the Yankees—face it), and one reason is that out there they don't have weather; they have a backdrop.

Now, a February wind whipping up from the river and funneling through the spaces between the skyscrapers (spaces, we call them streets, where I bloody well have to *walk*) can provide a bit more reality orientation than we absolutely need, but the nice thing about winter is that it's followed by spring (I recognize that this thought is not original with me). To remind them of human insignificance, Angelenos have only the impending earthquake they don't quite believe in; New Yorkers have the seasons.

Sometimes, however, it gets a little hard to tell them apart.

New Yorkers neither feel the ground frost softening beneath the sidewalks nor watch raccoon toddlers trying out the world beyond their winter nests. Instead we find urban emblems for the seasons. My summer begins with the first Good Humor man and my winter with the opening of the Wollman Skating Rink. Spring is here when asparagus shows up at the neighborhood fruit stand.

There are places where one can find asparagus year-round, but I always get nosebleeds when I shop in them. I'm too used to being called "buddy" to be comfortable with "sir," and anyway, at $4.29 a pound, "sir" isn't enough. "Your Highness," maybe.

Still, there *is* the annual asparagus glut, a sort of continuing Aprilfest. Great fat stalks steamed and slathered with butter, crisp cold ones with olive oil and sherry vinegar, bite-sized pieces stir-fried with soy and garlic, lemony cream of asparagus soup, and on and on and on and on. . . . All too soon, in a flurry of 59-cent specials, they disappear. But while they're around, we—being New Yorkers—can manage to get in some splendid fights about them. Gulliver's Big Endians and Little Endians were as babies mild compared to asparagus disputants. I know that the sensitive and sensible among you will be shocked to hear this, but there are some people who actually like *thin* asparagus.

I know, I know. It seems impossible. Nevertheless, it's true. To all outward appearances, Reader, they are as sane as you and I. But if you send them out shopping, they will pass by the majestic kings and queens of asparagusdom and return home with a sackful of scrawny reeds. "The big ones," they will say, oblivious to reality, "are woody."

Oh, false canard! oh, foul aspersion!! The big ones, you patiently explain, are perhaps woody on the bottom, but they are *ambrosial* on top. All one has to do is break them off precisely at the point God planned you to (the spot where the stalk gives a satisfying snap), and you are left with the most wonderful of paradoxes: a *substantial* tenderness.

But do these people care? No. They profess themselves appalled by the waste; the sight of you wantonly discarding two-thirds of an asparagus stalk shrivels their meager Calvinist souls. They would rather eke out their economical pleasure than plunge boldly into the recurring wonder of spring. (Some— among them my wife and the editor of this book—flat-out claim that skinny ones taste better, but they're just being perverse.) If Randy Newman wanted to do something useful for the world, he would write a song about them; short people probably *got* that way from eating scrawny asparagus.

Ah, well. Perhaps I go too far. I will think of spring and let the asparagus of human kindness flow through my veins. Besides, New York is not that far-off city where the imperfect is intolerable. Skinny-asparagus people got some reason to live: If they shop early, it's easier for the rest of us to find the good stuff. Which is, let me tell you, infinitely easier than growing the good stuff. But unfortunately, asparagus is not the only harbinger of spring, for even before the last professional football players have finished bashing each other around, the indoor air resounds to the merry thump of seed catalogs sliding through our mail slot and landing in the hall. Like the sap, our stupidity rises, and we begin to plan our garden.

Actually, there's nothing stupid about planning a garden, but actually attempting to grow one is a clear sign of city dweller's hubris. I certainly have never understood that song from *The Fantasticks* about the relative difficulties of children and vegetables, the one where the singer mysteriously feels that the latter are less trouble. This is nonsense. While it's true that radishes rarely stay out past midnight and make you call the neighbors to look for them, I've yet to have a child eaten by rabbits.

Nevertheless, every spring we imagine the harvest. This is the pleasant part of gardening; then Blaise Laspia comes around with his tractor to turn over about 1500 square feet of what we laughingly call "the lawn," and grim reality sets in. For some reason, I seem to be the one member of the household not entirely bemused by harvest fantasies; my imagination—and my memory—damn well encompass the physical agony of horticulture. My idea of the perfect garden is the one Mrs. Bartilucci runs with great efficiency just down the road; it comes complete with a stand, a scale, and a tin box for making change. With that and a small patch of herbs, my world would be complete. If I really wanted to injure my back, I could just go out on a tennis court and continue to mis-hit my overhead.

But when garden fever strikes, no citizen is safe. And it is, I admit, seductive. I can be in the living room turning the pages of a trashy novel, apparently insulated from any thought of manual labor, when a snatch of conversation about lettuce will float in from the gathering at the dining-room table. I somehow find myself forsaking Inspector Dalgleish and listening. I realize they aren't going to plant enough romaine. I get up. I enter the conversation. I pick up *Crockett's Victory Garden*. Against all my better judgment, I talk about what we will plant. Which means I am morally committed to weeding. I am so goddamn dumb.

No so dumb, however, that I want to do any more work than absolutely necessary. This means I am foursquare in favor of black plastic between the rows. Black plastic—available at your local nursery in handy rolls—prevents weeds from choking off the things you *want* to grow. It's wonderful.

But it is not beautiful. There are people, some of them partners in the garden, who reject this utilitarian mulch on aesthetic bases. (Also there's some long-run question about what it does to the soil, but I prefer to keep the conversation narrowed to grounds where I can wax righteous.) We argue. We argue, in fact, with some passion. It is suggested that weeding is good exercise. It is further suggested that the merest glance at my stomach is enough to identify me as someone who needs such exercise. My reply, I fear, is not itself very kind. In fact, if any tender shoots wandered into the dining room they would instantly turn brown and keel over.

A sudden stroke of genius: I yield on the matter of black plastic. Dramatically, I resign from the garden. I will be glad to cook whatever crops come up, but I will bear no responsibility whatsoever for their nurture. I leave the room, a study in injured dignity. I return to the quiet flipping of corpse-strewn pages.

And then I hear them talking about raspberry bushes. I don't think two will be quite enough, not if I'm going to be making fresh raspberry mousses. I put down the book. . . .

I mulch, I weed, I fall upon the thorns of life and bleed. That's an exaggeration (though I did get stung by a bee once, when I was rooting around in the snow peas, which doesn't really count), but it's understandable, for the peace of the Augustans—April's neat straight rows of shoots and seedlings—invariably gives way to Romantic excess. No matter how we try to work it out, the same thing happens every year: the garden goes berserk. The labor, planning, and domestic disputes that went into it bear fruit—and vegetables—to the extent that "ready for harvest" is a macabre understatement. The damn garden *explodes,* and we are in trouble.

The spinach comes first; notwithstanding any number of dishes Florentine, some of it goes to seed before we can use it. And of course every spinach salad defers the lettuce, so despite the household's best collective Bugs Bunny imitation, much of the lettuce goes the same route.

Next, the beets threaten. Quietly, as is their underground wont, they arrive at perfection. They are firm, sweet, and perhaps a couple of inches in diameter. They are also, to use a somewhat more poignant measure, in two thirty-foot rows. With about forty feet of beets to go, pride turns to horror. If we ate beets three times a day, we couldn't keep up. Invariably the last ones are surly and fibrous by the time they're uprooted.

Each beet root, of course, comes with its attendant greens; such is nature's cunning way. And when beet greens are freshly picked they are so delicious that one can't throw them away. (They are also seductively easy to prepare. Just wash 'em, put 'em in a colander, and slowly pour over them the water you've cooked the beets in. Add butter. Eat.)

But when the apparently modest beet thus provides both of the evening vegetables, does the rest of the garden slow down? Not on your life. The beans, both bush and string, are by then in high-production mode (and if they aren't picked and eaten when they're small, we might as well just buy week-old "fresh" ones at the supermarket); the yellow squash is almost ready; there are what look to be acres of Swiss chard; the spaghetti squash is bulging alarmingly; and at my back I always hear August's tomato-glut hurrying near.

I haven't, you will notice, so much as mentioned the zucchini. You may think this is because I choose to let sleeping zucchini lie, but this is not the case. First of all, there is no such thing as a sleeping zucchini; you never really catch them at it, but the little buggers are always growing. Pick a zucchini bush clean for supper, and by breakfast it'll be full again. Really.

And if you *don't* pick it, things are worse. For if the wee green perpetual-production machine isn't diverted into making tender new zucchini, it puts its energies into the ones it's currently bearing and turns them into MONSTERS. Overnight, a single zucchini can grow four inches. And does. This is a problem: a six-inch zucchini is heartrendingly delicious; at ten inches, it is suitable only for use as a bowling pin or a blunt instrument.

So you see what I'm up against. And I don't want to imply for a minute that the garden experts ever overplant, but there does come a time every summer when we eat God's own plenty of zucchini. There are deep-fried zucchini sticks, sausage-stuffed zucchini boats, stir-fried zucchini and onions, zucchini and radish salad with sour cream, zucchini pancakes, and just about every variation on zucchini known to person. So you can imagine the breakthrough it was when—in a desperate search through the cookbooks for yet another zucchini disguise—I found a recipe for zucchini blossoms.

As your basic Brooklynite, I'd never really thought about eating zucchini blossoms (they're extremely perishable and rarely make it to the city), but I knew one thing: If you eat a flower, it can't turn into a fruit. Quickly calculating folks' stomach capacities, I figured that everyone could knock back three or four zucchini blossoms, and that a dinner for eight could eliminate some thirty potential zucchini. Inspired by that, I really didn't care how the things tasted, but I'm pleased to report that the experience was every bit as luxurious as eating a flower ought to be. They were at once rich, light, and startlingly beautiful.

I was considerably less pleased to discover that the harvester studied up on how to distinguish the male blossoms from the female (there is a way, but I don't think we should talk about it in front of the children) and frugally picked only the male. Which never turn into fruits anyway. I think next year I'll suggest a rose garden.

You can never have too many roses (unless, I suppose, you're allergic to them, but that's as private a taste as fist-fucking, and I'm not going to let your aberration muck up my perfectly good generalization). They're pretty, you don't have to eat them, and the bees would probably hang around the front porch anyway. And when roses finally pack it in for the winter ("Oh, rose, thou art blown"), there's a great deal of sentimental foofaraw ("The Last Rose of Summer," sniffle, sniffle), and it's time to go back to school.

Tomatoes are not like roses. First of all, they're easier on the gardener. They don't demand heartless pruning and heaping bags of soil-enricher; you just crank 'em up and let 'em go. If you start out with reasonably healthy plants and don't actively maltreat them, you will be rewarded with tomatoes.

Or maybe punished. Perhaps because of melancholy experience with roses, home gardeners tend to have an overfatalistic approach to planting other things (see *zucchini*, above), and it is the careful husbandperson indeed who isn't awash in tomatoes by the beginning of August.

The annual tomato flood lasts, barring droughts or hurricanes, for about six weeks, by the end of which there is no longer any such thing as a Tomato Surprise. Instead, there have been fried green tomatoes, an inordinate number of things Italiano or Provençal, and—for the ants among us—great vats of tomato sauce put up against the winter. (For the grasshoppers, there have been tomato fights.)

By summer's end, in short, tomatoes are often viewed with a

profound skepticism, for they illustrate the classic hallmarks of the phenomenon economists describe as "declining marginal utility." Which is their clever way of saying that the season's first tomato, plucked warm from the plant and eaten while one stands in the garden admiring tomatoes to come, is clearly preferable—though identical in every measurable respect—to the season's last. The final rose petal flutters to the ground, and there is an epiphany about the transience of beauty; when the tomato plants cease production, there's dancing in the streets.

This is both unfair to the tomato, which is round and doesn't have thorns, and shortsighted. All too soon, the consumer who's been sticking out his tongue and making rude noises at the tomato patch is going to be faced with those pale-pink rocks that supermarkets import from underground mines in California. These make handsome paperweights, but lousy sauce. And they're gaining on us.

Perhaps it takes a curious summer like this one, when cool weather has held the tomatoes back, to make one overcome the prejudice of Augusts past, but I hope I have—that when they come, even in quantity, I will treasure each one as though it were summer itself. The time is short already, for November comes in on the first this year, and how the wind doth ram-oh.

CREAM OF FRESH PEA SOUP

1. Cook 1½ to 2 lbs. peas, shelled, and 1 large, chopped, Spanish onion, together with a moderate dollop of curry powder, in 1 qt. winy chicken stock until tender.

2. Pour off and reserve about half the stock; puree the peas, onions, and remaining stock in a blender or food processor until the peas are almost completely liquefied. If the puree appears unduly thick, add a bit more of the reserved stock.

3. Add 1 cup heavy cream and either reheat the soup and serve it immediately or chill it quite thoroughly for use as a cold soup.

If you decide for cold, the soup will probably need both additional curry and a dose of salt.

4. Top each bowl (hot or cold) with a little chopped watercress and a few healthy grinds from the peppermill.

5. Pray that June comes in on the first next year.

DEEP-FRIED ZUCCHINI BLOSSOMS

1. Sift ⅔ cup flour into mixture of 1 large, beaten egg and ¾ cup water, stirring constantly. If it begins to look any thicker than sour cream, stop adding flour.

2. Cut one side of each blossom open, remove the stamen, and open the flower to flatten it slightly.

3. Heat about 1 inch of cooking oil in a heavy frying pan until it is very hot. Dip each blossom into the batter and add them, a few at a time, to the pan.

4. Cook them until the undersides are brown (about 30 seconds), then turn them over for a similar length of time. Remove them, drain on paper towels, sprinkle on a little coarse salt, and serve quickly.

GRILLED TOMATOES

As your basic grasshopper type, I've never been able to get seriously involved in the autumnal mass production of sauces. This is a character flaw, I know, but it's mine own. For me, the tomato makes its last stand grilled. It can of course be served absolutely plain, with perhaps a little melted butter drizzled over it in the manner of an English mixed grill, but there is a peculiarly melancholy joy to be achieved by wedding the last tomatoes with the end of the summer's basil. It's both easy and elegant to put a spoonful of pesto sauce atop the little hollow where the core has been removed and run the tomato under the broiler for a couple of minutes. Equally good, and slightly quicker, is a topping composed of butter, breadcrumbs, grated Parmesan, and basil blended in the following proportions: 2 tablespoons each of the first three ingredients and 4 tablespoons coarsely chopped basil.

Q: What's White and Hairy and Sweet All Over? A: Don't Ask.

The family tradition that the birthday celebrant gets to choose the dinner (and doesn't have to wash the dishes) goes back as far as I can remember. Hamburgers were what I mostly picked. The ritual continues, at least as far as yesterday, which was the Mad Baker's sixteenth birthday. He chose clams and champagne.

I thought this was a swell choice (*very* fuckin' sophisticated, y'know), and mentioned it—well, bragged about it, actually—to an uptown editor with whom I was doing a little business. She responded with a tale involving an elderly woman, very much the grande dame, whose debilitating and perhaps terminal illness prevented her from continued piggery at the table. It apparently didn't interfere with her sense of quality, however, for one day at the Colony, she lunched on an oyster, a raspberry, and a glass of champagne. Sigh.

Lacking any suitable fancy illness, we bought five dozen clams for the four of us. Half were just raw, with lemon and Louisiana hot sauce, and we ran the other half under the broiler as clams casino. Those that we had cooked were spectacular—plumped by the heat, soaked in garlic butter, and topped with crisp bacon; they were welcomed with glad hosannas. The raw ones, however, were another story.

Maybe they were a little on the tired side and the problem was the fish market's (though we've often shopped there before), or maybe even a sixteenth birthday isn't enough to let you get away with declaring summer in the middle of February. They were okay, but that's all, and birthday dinners really should be magic. You can't fool Mother Nature.

Not that you should get all worked up worrying about us; I mean, it takes a special kind of chutzpah to complain that one's clams and champagne weren't perfect, right? But the mild disappointment did get me to thinking about seasonal foods. I suppose that if the birthday boy had asked for corn on the cob, we would have served it, but it would take a lot of traditional weight before a request of that sort would be honored. Fresh corn in winter—or in the city during any season—is always less good than one remembers it.

Parsnips, however, are something else. Obviously. No one has ever mistaken a parsnip for an ear of corn. Though you can make cream of parsnip soup. You can also make parsnip pie; I never have, but the brilliantly revised—which is to say, restored—*Fannie Farmer Cookbook* has an absolutely fascinating recipe soon to turn up for dessert. Fascinating, that is, if you like parsnips.

Unlike birthday dinners, parsnips were not a tradition in my family. In fact, to my knowledge, they were never even a flash in the pan. I think that had to do with the invention of frozen vegetables, a phenomenon that hit just about as I was moving off pablum. For the first time in their lives (and mine too, but it was less dramatic for me), my parents didn't have to make it through the winter on root vegetables. So they didn't.

They had, after all, endured years and years of parsnips, turnips, and rutabagas appearing in turn on February plates. After a while, even canned peas looked pretty good to them, and frozen were a miracle. So by the time I discovered the splendors of the parsnip, it was as exotic to me as the kiwi fruit. Cheaper, too.

I sort of backed into my discovery by way of those preassembled packages of soup vegetables that show up on supermarket shelves; usually it's a leek or onion, a carrot or two, some celery, some parsley, and some dill. But every now and then, there's a parsnip in the pack.

The first thing I noticed about this vegetable (whose name I did not then know) was its smell. Cut open a parsnip, breathe in, and it's like walking through a rainsoaked hayfield. The smell is a sweet and earthy reminder of summers past and a promise of summers to come. And at the tail end of winter, parsnips are at their best; it's true—the sugar concentrates as they slowly shrink and grow dense during their long storage period. And they are very easy to cook. You just peel and slice them like carrots (julienne, rather than rounds), and steam them until tender (about 10 minutes). Then, fine words availing naught, you slather them with butter and a handful of chopped parsley. Makes you think winter's not so bad after all.

Beach Banquet Bingo

I have long regarded the beach as the penalty one pays for going swimming. Water is swell, especially great crashing waves for romping, but not beaches. In my ideal world, the breakers would foam right up to a cool green lawn, liberally dotted with shade trees. There I would sit, unbothered by the sun's glare, and allow the breezes to ruffle my remaining hair as I turned the pages of a trashy novel. Occasionally—very occasionally—I would get up to play in the waves. I would never burn the soles of my feet on the way to the water and never get sand down my bathing suit. And of course I would never do whatever it is people have in mind when they announce that they are going to "work on" their tans.

I'm not fooling. I mean, sometimes I use this column to joke around a little, right? Not today. For the last ten summers I've lived within comfortable walking distance of a beach, and I've gone swimming in the daylight maybe twice a year. Nighttime is the right time.

I'm told that all this sometimes makes me a drag to live with. Indeed, I have sometimes been told this so forcefully that I've packed up my prejudices in my old kit bag and gone to the beach, where I've curled myself into a snarling sulky ball and spoiled everybody's afternoon. This is not a mere tactic (though it does rather discourage invitations), but a sort of beachophobic self-fulfilling prophecy. I go there expecting to have a miserable time, and by God, I do.

Having thus established my tastes quite firmly in the minds of my nearest and dearest, I confidently expected that this summer would be pretty much like all others, and that while some folk were off at the beach, I would be devoting myself to the inaccurate bashing of tennis balls. I erred. In fact, I erred severely, underestimating the cleverness of the twin appeal to which I would be subjected, for my usual temptation to follow the Woman Warrior to the ends of the earth (or at least to Sagaponack) was cleverly exploited by one of the house's other residents: the all-time World Champion beach person, Potatoes O'Brian.

For most of the year the deceptively mild-mannered O'Brian is a man of simple needs: a little beer, a little Scotch, a little dope, and a large jar of Skippy Creamy Peanut Butter is to him Paradise Enow. But in the summer he goes beach-crazy, trading in his healthy barroom pallor for an unsuitable shade of red, which I'm sure is bad for him.

But to give the devil his due, your man O'Brian knows how to go to the beach. Actually, now that I think about it, "go" is really the wrong verb; he doesn't so much visit the beach as relocate to it. O'Brian packs for an afternoon's sun and surf with an attention to detail that makes Eisenhower's approach to the Normandy landing seem positively casual.

So there they were, the two of them, making lists and checking them twice, while I maintained a dignified indifference to the entire proceeding—until I was co-opted by clams. Along with hamburgers and hot dogs to cook on the hibachi, O'Brian proposed taking along a few dozen clams. This struck me as a pleasant enough idea, and I volunteered to whip up a molten cocktail sauce. With that first step, my doom was sealed. When the Woman Warrior reminded us that she didn't particularly care for raw clams, I pointed out that we could cook a dozen or so for her right on the grill. (It's easy: Just put the clams on over a hot fire, and when the shells pop open, throw in a dollop of butter and lemon juice. Delicious.)

Next thing you know, I'm traipsing across the sand, dragging a twenty-pound bag of charcoal. I'm lighting the fire, smoking dope, eating clams, drinking beer (O'Brian has a commodious cooler, of course), in the shade of a beach umbrella. The umbrella is a *terrific* idea; why haven't we done this before? This is a great afternoon. I can hardly wait to do it again.

O'Brian and the Woman Warrior follow up on their advantage. Each visit brings with it the promise of some new delight. Madder music and hotter sauce. By the time we start roasting ears of corn in the charcoal (put 'em right in the coals, turning them once or twice, for about ten minutes; when you peel back the charred husks, the kernels will be incredibly plump and moist), I'm a confirmed beach person. As long as there's an umbrella. And some clams, and some beer, and some dope. . . .

Sweet Smell of Excess

Vacation time, sort of. We are demonstrating the Youngest Member to her many grandparents, who live—to our great good fortune—on the Cape. But if Cape Cod is an almost perfect symbol of "vacation," the Youngest Member is the essence of "sort of." She doesn't really understand the *concept* of vacation (nor, for that matter, the concept of "concept"). We are looking for a break in the daily routine, but she is putting all her tiny effort into establishing one.

As you might imagine, this conflict produces a certain testiness. Though she is remarkably tolerant the first nine times the brakes slam on and the car swerves to a halt, the tenth antique shop produces an unstoppable torrent of tears and recriminations. I understand; I get a little tired of Sandwich glass after a while myself. But while the car's motion eventually works to calm her down, I miss a mile or so of shops, and one of them—I *know* it—has just what I'm looking for.

She gets her revenge in the mornings. Which is why, at dawn last Thursday, I was staring glumly out my mother's living-room window rather than having pleasant dreams of fifty-cent Rookwood vases at garage sales.

Behind me, from the convertible couch, there were these absurdly charming piglet noises—great rootings and suckings and sighs of contentment. Before me was a cup of reheated coffee and the hope that the Youngest Member might nurse herself back to sleep. There was also an animal.

It was moseying along the edge of the tall grass some twenty yards from the window, and I had never seen anything like it before. Actually, I had seen something like it, because at first I thought it was a raccoon. On the other hand, I also thought it was a rabbit.

I was mistaken, but the error was understandable, for what stood out in the half-light certainly appeared to be a rabbit's head. A classic, snow-white bunny, dipping up and down into the tall grass. Bunny ears and everything. But bunnies, I knew, were not in the habit of traveling around with packs on their back. If this was a rabbit, it was dragging a large sack behind it. Perhaps, I thought, there was a gang of robber bunnies working the Cape during the summer, but this seemed unlikely—I mean, my mother would have said something about it, don't you think?

So instead of disturbing the Youngest Member's breakfast with the news that a robber bunny was loose outside, I prudently chose—you go around announcing that killer rabbits are attacking your house and people will begin to think you're not fit to be President—to polish my glasses and look again. "Jesus," I said, "there's a skunk in the yard."

"Mmmrph?" said the Woman Warrior.

"A skunk. In the yard."

Rustle of bedclothes, swish of 1940s pajamas (*very* Katharine Hepburn, very sexy), warm presence beside me. "A skunk," she agreed.

"In the yard," I added. "Close to us."

There's not, it turns out, much you can *do* about a skunk in the yard. Marauding rabbits, you can Take Steps; skunks, you watch. And you reminisce a little. Trips to the children's zoo, cross-crountry drives where the smell hit like a wet slap, the time Lizzie the Dog mistakenly chased a skunk and how funny she looked when you were washing her with tomato juice . . . but that's about it. All in all, a skunk in the yard encourages a certain passivity, and I suppose I'm grateful to the Youngest Member for leading me to discover the perfect vacation animal.

~~~~~~~~

SAUTÉED CABBAGE WITH ROSEMARY

Like a skunk, cabbage often gets bad-rapped for its smell; tough-guy detectives are always tracking down minor hoods in some "boarding house where even the faded roses on the wallpaper reek of last year's boiled cabbage." But even Philip Marlowe, hot on the trail of a killer rabbit, might pause for this seasonal dish.

1. Quarter and core 1 small, firm cabbage. Cut the quarters as though you were making coleslaw. Rinse the cabbage ribbons in cold water and drain.

2. Melt 2 tablespoons butter in an equal amount of olive oil over low heat in a heavy, coverable skillet. When the butter has liquefied, add the cabbage, stir thoroughly to coat, and cover the pot. Stir again in about 5 minutes.

3. When the cabbage has softened only slightly (about another 5 minutes), uncover the pot, and sprinkle the cabbage with 2 generous tablespoons fresh rosemary leaves (or a scant tablespoon of dried ones, previously softened in a little warm water, which should also go into the cabbage with them). Increase the heat to high, add more oil and butter if necessary, and sauté the cabbage briskly; it may brown, but rapid stirring will keep it from burning.

Hooray for Holidays

A warm spring evening, one of the year's first, and this middle-aged man's fancy was essaying a few libidinous pirouettes. The Woman Warrior's reading lamp was still on, but she was snuggled into me and purring noises against my chest. Suddenly she jerked her head up and spoke, "I wonder what kind of candy we should get for her Easter basket?"

"Wha-a-a-t?? *Easter* baskets? Why didn't you just wait a minute or two, and then you could've complained that the ceiling needs painting."

My outrage was rewarded with a giggle and a tweak, but we did eventually return to the question of the Youngest Member's first-ever Easter basket, during which conversation I realized the Woman Warrior is one of those people who thinks holidays are "*really* for the children"—a position I abandoned about the time I started shaving. Holidays are for *me*.

I admit there really isn't a whole lot in the world that is as much fun as sharing a three-year-old's Christmas, but I find that a huge stack of presents all addressed to me comes very close indeed. Even a small stack isn't bad. I suppose that's why Christmas is my favorite holiday. I can't offhand think of a bad one, though, and even those traditional patriotic festivals that could turn mean in a hurry during Vietnam were often redeemed by something as simple as an earnest drum-and-bugle corps.

Tradition, in a word, is comforting—unless, of course, that tradition happens to be plum pudding. After all, flogging was for many years a British Navy ritual, but those who had to endure it didn't get all dewy-eyed over its passing. And though eating Christmas plum pudding is not an unpleasantness of quite the same order as being flayed, I don't know a single person who deep-down honest likes it—who would, for instance, willingly pick it off the Four Seasons' dessert cart on a February evening. Imagine, if you will, amid the delicate mousses and buttery pastries, a nasty lump of plum pudding. There it sits, a collection of poisonously tinted dried fruits, forcibly joined by a glutinous boiled dough. And there it would continue to sit through the changing seasons until some holiday-addled sucker went for it on Christmas future—at which time, to be fair, it would taste no worse than it would have ten months earlier. Though all manner of good things spoil, plum pudding is virtually indestructible. By me, this does not count in its favor.

In a better world, plum pudding would by now have gone the way of the passenger pigeon, and if I thought the dreaded dessert was actually on the way out, I'd devote these holiday thoughts to organizing my Christmas list. I do not, after all, want to beat a dead horse (itself, I assure you, more appetizing than the typical plum pudding). But no. In an awesome tribute to the power of nostalgia to cloud men's minds, every damn newspaper in the country spends Thanksgiving vacation rummaging through its files so it can start December with its very own hopeless recipe for plum pudding.

At first the national fascination with plum pudding may seem simply curious, but it's a logical effect of the secular age. Absent religion, Christmas threatens to degenerate into a celebration of the Mattel Toy Company. This will not do. The firm no doubt has virtues that deserve a quick tip of the hat, but these would hardly justify an annual month-long binge. Hence, plum pudding.

I don't want, by this analysis, to blame plum pudding on the liberals; what with the Moral Majority and Norman "The Frother" Podhoretz, they've got enough to worry about. (Besides, the return of the Inquisition seems a heavy price to pay for even the merriest Christmas.) Liberals may have catalyzed the pro-plum-pudding movement, but they are hardly its cause. The search for tradition is stronger than partisanship, and in the absence of anything so resoundingly Dickensian as plum pudding (Dickens having by now replaced the Evangelists as the holiday's prime definer), the fruity lump is fated to appear on the Christmas table, then to linger in a remote corner of the fridge until spring cleaning, when it will be chucked out and give a hernia to some unsuspecting sanitation man who thinks the garbage pail contains merely its usual complement of empty beer bottles. Even in April plum pudding is infinitely more blessed to give than to receive.

Don't get me wrong—I'd rather get presents and endure plum pudding than escape it and get none—but the absence of the stuff is a strong point in Flag Day's favor. There are, in fact, lots of okay lootless holidays. May Day provides the odd combo of Commies and hyperdulia, St. Patrick's Day guarantees bagpipes and drunken teen-agers, and Thanksgiving is so positively weird there's something affecting about it. I mean, a whole day devoted to gluttony; that's *weird*. High school football's part of the ritual too, I suppose, but it's hardly as central as serious piggery.

The moralists who annually complain about American overindulgence in a starving world are right, of course, but they miss the point. Excess is Thanksgiving's historical *raison d'être*, but it's justified, I think, less from its roots than from the special role it plays in the atomized American present; it is the chief occasion in the year when family recipes are brought forth, and we acknowledge—in a particularly direct way—our position as descendants.

Now, even that tradition may be giving way. Restaurant meals, thanks to the lethal wonders of microwave ovens, are of course growing ever more anonymous, but home cooking—

even, or perhaps especially, "serious" home cooking—is changing as well. Given the shifts in domestic patterns and demographics, increasing numbers of people are learning to cook, not at the family stove, but in the cramped kitchens of their first apartments. From books. Though the metaphor—not to mention the reality—would no doubt disconcert them both, Julia and Craig are Ma and Pa to many a fledgling cook.

Which isn't all that bad, mind you; it just makes for predictable eating. Home-cooked meals *ought* to be a trifle quirky; one should be able to taste the cook's eccentricities and heritage. So while there's nothing wrong with Claiborne's suggestions (or James Beard's, or any responsible cookbook writer's), to follow them rather than one's family is to change Thanksgiving from a holiday that links the generations and thus to remove an irrefutable counterclaim to the moralists' antipiggery complaints.

That said, I'd like to talk a little bit about my mother's stuffing recipe. It was also, fittingly, *her* mother's recipe. And her mother's mother's. Before that, I don't know. Indeed, I trace it to my great-grandmother only by an odd circumstance in family history. Or maybe not so odd when you think about it, for into each marriage come two stuffing recipes: one maternal, one paternal. Usually, one of them gives way. And usually, at least at a time when women had charge of the kitchen, it was the maternal line that survived. My grandfather, however, was by all accounts a cantankerous sort, and my grandmother, herself pretty stubborn, wound up making two stuffings every year. One end of the bird was filled with *his* mother's potato stuffing, the other with *her* mother's traditional New England bread stuffing.

This arrangement, while superficially fair, had its drawbacks: The cook wound up slogging through twice as much work (of the most boring kind), and whichever stuffing went into the breast cavity missed out on most of the delicious turkey juices that any stuffing needs if it's to taste as good as it used to. It would be going too far to say this bipolar turkey *caused* their marriage to fall apart, but I bet it didn't help matters any. My grandfather apparently got custody of the potato stuffing after the breakup, for it has disappeared from the family repertoire—a good thing, probably, as I'm not sure how succeeding generations would have coped with marriages involving two people and three stuffings. The Estragon/Warrior stuffing treaty—one year, her cornbread-and-sausage; the next, my bread—seems fairer to the signatories, but I sometimes wonder if it will eventually confuse our grandchildren; heirlooms tie us not only to the past but to the future.

To some extent, then, keeping a family holiday is a burden as well as a pleasure, and there are surely times when one might be forgiven a sharp "What has posterity done for *me* lately?" But there are many when one would not.

For instance, on the last Christmas before the Youngest Member was born, her arrival was so imminent that we thought it safer to assemble all the various relatives in Brooklyn than to journey away from our midwife. During the afternoon, with the rib roast making enticing noises from the oven, I briefly fled the kitchen and went out on the front porch for a while. I was a little stoned, it's true (we'd given the boys some rainbow rolling papers in their stockings, and they'd invited me down to their lair for a multicolored toke), but nothing could have been quite so disorienting as the weather. I was standing there in my shirtsleeves, thinking vaguely about how nice the morning had been, when I heard this out-of-season *thwunk*. It was the unmistakable sound of a baseball smacking into a leather glove; the boys were playing catch. For a moment, I envied the moral suppleness of youth. Like me, they'd lamented the absence of snow, but if some celestial jokester had decided December 25 was going to be spring, they were prepared to take advantage of it. I was merely befuddled.

Just then, Santa came out of the Zuckers' house next door. That was nice; I didn't expect that. Neither did my nieces. They were nine and five, and while the older had become a skeptic about Santa, the five-year-old remained a true believer. They spun away from the boys and watched pop-eyed as Santa made his way down the front steps and headed for the sidewalk. Obligingly, his eyes atwinkle through his tiny rimless glasses, he put his finger beside his nose and said, "Hello, little girls." They were too amazed to reply, and stared silently as Santa crossed the street to the Napolis' house. He didn't bother ringing the bell, just ho-ho-ho'd right in.

Thwunk. The catch game, briefly interrupted by the stately passage of Mr. Claus, resumed. The little girls no longer paid attention, though; they were focused entirely on the Napolis' door. If Santa went *in*, he'll come *out*, right?

Well, maybe. Maybe for all I knew, Santa was working his way through Brooklyn, house-by-house. In which case we could be next. I went inside to tell people. "I just saw Santa Claus," I announced. "I think he's on the way here."

No response. My in-laws, who'd long harbored doubts about me, exchanged meaningful glances and went back to their books; everybody else was caught in fierce concentration over some sort of computer game. I felt like jumping up and down and screaming, "I did, I did," but I decided that would be silly. I also decided I was maybe a little more stoned than I thought, so I decided to cool it and go open some clams. Clams are reliable.

I was out in the kitchen telling the clams about Santa when the little girls burst into the house. They were embroiled in a hot dispute about whether that was *really* Santa. The five-year-old, near tears, insisted it was; her coolly superior sister proclaimed it was just someone in a costume. Scornfully, she capped her argument, "If that was really Santa, where are his reindeer?"

This was not a bad question, and if anyone had paid attention to me when I'd told them Santa was walking around outside, I might have raised it myself. Not because I didn't think he was real or anything like that, only as a matter of curiosity. But I could tell it had the five-year-old worried.

Miraculously the computer game stopped buzzing and whirring, and the new Christmas books slammed shut as the adults rallied round to repair the fragile net of plausibility. It turned out that reindeer can't land when there's no snow on the ground, and that an elf had them circling around the distant sky, waiting to pick Santa up when he was ready to go.

"But"—the nine-year-old Socrates again—"what's he doing here at all? If he already brought the presents, why isn't he back in the North Pole?" Well, that's because every year, when his work is done, a tired Santa picks one lucky family and visits them for Christmas dinner. Then when he has his strength back, he climbs in his sleigh and heads home for another year.

This modification of tradition seemed satisfactory, and as the theologians mulled it over, the doorbell rang. If this is Santa, I thought as I hurried to it, I sure hope he's not drunk. But it wasn't. It was four young believers, one of whom—a blond boy whose enthusiasm for his bicycle exceeds his control of it—I recognized. "Hey, mister," he said, "did Santa Claus come to this house?"

"Not since last night."

"But did you see him *today?*"

I thought for a minute, then said gravely, "Yes."

MY MOTHER'S GRANDMOTHER'S
TURKEY STUFFING

For a 14-lb. bird, pick a loaf and a half of somewhat stale, unsliced white bread into small irregular chunks. (This is, my mother points out, an activity that is bound to make you feel stupid. Ignore it.) When the white is picked out, soak the crusts briefly in water, wring them out, and tear them into similar small pieces. Mix the crumbed bread together with at least 3 or 4 chopped large onions, and pour in ½ lb. melted butter. Mix it in well, using your hands, and add Bell's seasoning until the stuffing tastes wonderful (lots of tasting here—best part of the operation). Let it cool, then stuff and roast.

Two notes: first, if you've neglected to buy bread enough ahead of time to let it get stale, you can achieve a satisfactory effect by puncturing the crust several times with a long-tined fork and letting the bread stand in a slow (200–degree) oven for a couple of hours. Second, in recent years I've slipped slightly away from family tradition and have been cooking capons instead of a turkey. There is no evidence that my great-grandmother minds.

~~~~~~~~

CLAMS CASINO

Allow between 4 and 6 cherrystone clams per person as a first course, a dozen as an entrée.

First, open the clams. This is the hard part; and can be described only with lots of diagrams. If you're feeding a batch of people (and if your fish market is open on the day you plan to cook), you might prudently buy them already shucked and on the half-shell. Cream together some salted butter, a great deal of garlic, and a modest amount of dried red pepper. Put about ½ teaspoon of this mixture on each clam, then cover each with a square of bacon. Broil, close to the flame, until the bacon crisps (about 2 minutes) and serve immediately, with plenty of good bread to soak up the extra juices.

Home Plates

I have a cold, of course, but that pretty much happens every spring and is my own damn fault. By now, I should know enough to dress in peelable and replaceable layers. Instead, I annually fall prey to overoptimism and wind up freezing after the sun goes down. A day later my nose begins to run.

But I'm not the only one confused by spring. Though the flowering cherry in the back yard is in full and glorious bloom, a glance at the television reveals that black persons in short pants are still doing amazing things with basketballs, and white folks on ice skates are losing their tempers and bashing each other with sticks. Don't they know there's a warm on? Don't they know there's *baseball?*

Mine was probably the last generation to be spared this messy overlap; in the days when I was forming my ill-fated attachment to the Red Sox, a certain order to the calendar enabled me to keep my fantasies nicely separate: in the fall, I was Charley Connerly; in winter, Bob Cousy; in spring and summer, Vern Stephens (and sometimes Dom DiMaggio, who wore glasses and hit a lot of doubles). So when I speared that tricky pickup deep in the hole ("Makes those tough plays look easy," said the announcer in my head admiringly), I was never tempted to feed

Bill Sharman cutting through the lane for an easy layup. Kids today have it hard. No wonder they're all dyeing their hair green and staying out too late. Fact is, any halfway competent statistician could demonstrate a strong positive correlation between the rise in teen-age suicides and the reckless expansion of sports' seasons. It's true. You could look it up.

I'm too old to be a teen-age suicide by now (and if the Red Sox didn't get me in '75 and '78, I'm probably going to make it through middle age). So the Knicks didn't actually save my life with their graceful El Foldo in the first round of the playoffs, but they did clear the mind wonderfully for the opening of baseball season.

Though the heavy drama of a pennant race doesn't grip the heart until fall (Reggie Jackson, no fool, is "Mr. October"; who would wish to be known as "Mr. April"?), spring's innocent exuberance makes for thrills of a more forgiving sort. Baseball, unlike life, actually wipes the slate clean every year, and even Cubs fans are allowed a few blessed weeks of April hope.

My own green dreams have shifted over the years—grown, I think, more catholic. Along about the time I saw my first curve ball, I realized I was never going to be even a high school player; an embarrassing number of years later, I finally admitted that the strength of my passion wasn't alone enough to propel the Red Sox into the Series. Now, the fever of partisanship has softened into gratitude that I'm still here and that they're still playing the game.

So we went out to Shea on the season's first weekend to watch a rite renewed. This was a mega-special occasion, for the Woman Warrior's parents were visiting us, and it was her mother's first trip ever to a major league game. She allowed as how it was pretty, and she was right. Real grass, bright sunlight, hot dogs, home runs, beer, peanuts ... we sat, three generations, in the upper deck, and root, root, rooted for the home team. To no avail, as it happened (the Mets have the potential to break as many hearts as the Red Sox), but we didn't mind. For an hour or so, we lost ourselves in the elegant geometry of the world between the foul lines. And when the Expos put on the Kingman shift—pulling their second baseman to the shortstop's side of the field—Ted Williams stepped out of memory's on-deck circle and took his place in my mind's batter's box; for that moment or two, I was again young enough to take each spring for granted. Then I sneezed.

BRAISED LAMB WITH JUNIPER BERRIES

An Easter lamb is as traditional a sign of spring in many cultures as baseball is in ours, but the annual Estragon nod to tradition was complicated this year by the presence of the Woman Warrior's parents. We generally either roast our legs of lamb or have the butcher bone and butterfly them for grilling over charcoal; in either case, we like the meat a rosy pink. Since rare lamb was anathema to the older generation—and well-done roast lamb an abomination to anyone—we opted for slow, moist cooking that allowed the lamb to be thoroughly done without drying out.

1. Have the butcher carefully trim most of the fat from the outside of a small (6 lb.) leg of lamb and crack the bone at the shoulder end and shank joint. About an hour before cooking, remove it from the refrigerator and salt and pepper the skin thoroughly.

2. Put the lamb in a heavy metal casserole, with a tight-fitting top, together with ½ bottle dry white wine, 1 finely chopped carrot, 1 small chopped onion, ½ rib chopped celery, 4 whole peeled cloves garlic, a handful of parsley, 1 teaspoon dried rosemary leaves, and 1 dozen juniper berries. Set the heat low, cover the casserole, and cook everything together for about 3 hours, turning the lamb every half hour or so. It's unlikely that you'll need more liquid—the lamb throws off a fair amount—but add more wine if required.

3. Remove the lamb and set it on a platter. Skim as much fat off the top of the cooking liquid as possible, and if it seems a little thin, reduce it over high heat. Strain and serve it as a sauce for the meat.

Where the
Angst Is

On Being
Flat-Chested

*A*n extraordinary number of years ago, when I was studying for my Ph.D. orals, my then wife honored the lunacy of those final desperate weeks by removing herself and the kids to her parents, thus freeing me to do nothing but work. I stayed in the apartment on East 6th Street, books and notes accreting around our one comfortable chair in tidy, and eventually untidy, heaps. In a few days, the living-room floor had become a sludge of literature, notes on the unreliable narrator as exemplified in *Wuthering Heights* all higgledy-piggledy with the linear links between *Beowulf* and *Njal Saga*. A neighbor came up to check in and say howdy, took one look, and vanished downstairs to tell his wife that I was in dire straits indeed: I hadn't shaved, I barely talked, etc., etc.

They decided the least they could do was feed me, and my neighbor's wife went out to buy some extra chopped meat for the spaghetti sauce already simmering on their stove. They also decided, given the shape I was in, not to interrupt me with their plan, but just to come upstairs and lead me to dinner when it was ready.

As night fell, I heard a knock on the door and stumbled down the hall to see her standing there. Before she could issue her invitation, I spoke: "Hi, Aleen. Come in. Come in. Come in. I

67

can't stand here right now—I'm just about to flame the cognac on the steak Diane."

"Oh," she said (rather blankly, I thought). "No, that's all right. I don't want to bother you if you're busy," and immediately started back down the stairs. I called after her to make sure she was feeling okay, then—a little mystified—returned to my kitchen.

I learned about their planned dinner invitation a couple of weeks later, and the story eventually became a thread in our carpet of neighborliness. Usually, it was played for laughs—sometimes as a mockery of the "poor helpless bachelor" notion, more often as a symbol of my ludicrous preoccupation with food. Because of that context, I suppose, I never got to tell them how much I would have preferred spaghetti in company to solitary steak. The only thing better than eating food someone you love has cooked for you is cooking for someone you love.

Almost always, cooking for my children has been like that. Divorced daddies all develop little tricks to see us through those early days when we fear we'll lose our kids' affections—the circus, unlimited late-night TV, McDonald's—but that's divorce carried on by other means. Eventually, at least if we're lucky, a rhythm sets in, and it becomes possible to offer love in less synthetic ways. After a while, the boys' expressions as they ate a dinner they really like became less an implied comparison with their absent mother, more an affirmation of a kind of love stretching back to their first baby bottles.

Which brings me to breasts. More particularly, to the fact that I have none, and the Woman Warrior has two. With the Youngest Member dining on nothing but breast milk, this radically unequal division—once, I admit, a source of considerable satisfaction—has come to seem unfair. If there are two breasts per household, each parent should have one.

But that's not the way it is (at least not in our house, and I'm not sure I believe that *Post* story about the guy who took hormones either). The Woman Warrior has these elegantly efficient feeding devices and gets to exchange beatific smiles with the Youngest Member during feeding times; I get to change the diapers.

And it's not even that I *mind* changing them (though if I told you it was my favorite thing, I'd be fibbing), it's just that I feel left out, useless, otiose, irrelevant. . . . I am baroque; the Woman Warrior is Bauhaus. My nipples are absurdly small, my chest uselessly hairy. I was actually more help during birth, when I could coach, than I am now. Why didn't Freud get me ready for *this?*

Probably, I suppose, because he was so aflutter about toilet training that the question of input never crossed his tiny Austrian mind. Well, fuck him. And Karen Horney too (I am an equal-opportunity hater). *Nobody* told me about this. All the baby books warned the Woman Warrior (in terms highly unflattering to fathers, by the way) that I would be jealous, but no one said I'd be envious.

Well, I am, and there's nothing to be done about it, no chemical combo can match breast milk. And since nothing man-made is yet good for the Youngest Member, there's no recipe for this page.

Haste Makes Dinner

A paradox, as we all know, is G. K. Chesterton standing on his head in order not to draw attention to himself; it is also a confirmed lollygagger like me pleading the virtues of efficiency. Saying a kind word for efficiency is difficult because the term invariably evokes an image of industrial engineers striding briskly through factories, clicking their stopwatches on and off as they make notes on their clipboards. You know, save a second here, a second there, and before you know it, you're General Motors. Or McDonald's. Unsafe at any speed.

But the ability to function efficiently in a kitchen—to turn out one's own "fast food"—is necessary in order to enjoy one of the traditional benefits of slow food: the dinner hour.

My own feelings about "having dinner," as distinct from just eating, range from the merely neurotic to the full-fledged nutty. Mostly because my father traveled a lot when I was young (it took me thousands of dollars, hundreds of fifty-minute hours, and scores of Kleenexes to figure this out; I'll just give you the short version). When he was away, my mother—eager for someone, anyone to talk to—used to eat dinner with me. But when my father came off the road, I was fed and bedded early, while my parents stayed up late to eat of various forbidden fruits.

So dinner, you see, has these *implications*. What it hasn't had for a number of years is lots of time to get it ready. Thus the dependable stew, the complicated casserole, and the other staples of bourgeois cuisine are often impossible, for they depend, after all, on the bourgeois family. While *Papa* is out at the *bureau de change* insulting tourists, *Maman* is filling her string bag with goodies and spending her long afternoon making lovely smells. This, needless to say, is not an accurate picture of life *chez* Estragon.

Before the birth of the Youngest Member, the Woman Warrior and I were usually off bullyragging politicians or poking through grimy documents. We arrived home to be greeted by feral grunts from the kids, whose afternoon intake (mostly pizza and potato chips) had already been converted into yet more astonishing growth. "Food," they growled, throwing their elongated bodies to the floor and nipping not so playfully at my ankles.

We dodged. We delayed. We demanded, finally, "at least a goddamn minute to sit down and have a glass of wine," and they slunk off to the television. That I didn't lay in a supply of frozen pot pies for such occasions was a product of my neurosis, I know, but I didn't. Instead, we had a baby.

This was not neurotic (I think), but it was sure inconvenient. One or the other of us was home during the day, true, but we weren't what you'd call productive. Indeed, until the Youngest Member began sleeping through the night, we were shell-shocked. And as she has grown more active, the parent who spends the day out in the world is greeted not only with husky shouts of "When's dinner?" but by an armful of warm baby rather desperately proffered by the stay-at-home.

Eventually, one of us staggers out to the kitchen and begins puttering. At which point we are forcefully reminded that the thrifty French housewife has gotten by with low-cost materials because she spends time working over them; when the nightly dinner is prepared under deadline pressure, food bills can get out of hand. It's quick and easy to broil a steak or some lamb chops, but this way lies penury. Also boredom. And you can bet we're not gonna be slicing up $400-a-pound truffles to give dinner a little extra zing. Necessity being the mother, I've learned a fair number of tricks to cope with late meetings and late-breaking stories, and when *The New York Times* started running Pierre Franey's "60-Minute Gourmet" column every Wednesday, I figured I could cop a few more goodies from him, but I decided he was a cheater.

In the first place, there was this notion that turning out dinner in an hour made Pierre one plucky feller. This is silly. If I had an hour in the kitchen every night, dinner would be your basic piece of cake. (It wouldn't, of course, *be* a piece of cake; I just got caught up in some vivid writing. I meant it would be easy.) Because you'll remember that the 60-minute gourmet never had to spend any time shopping. He just walked into the kitchen and picked up the Cornish game hens that happened to be in the fridge, along with the fresh tarragon and asparagus, and whipped through a few basic routines.

Life is not like that. In real life, failure to shop produces a refrigerator that is empty of everything except ice cubes. Such a refrigerator allows one to make a cooling, but not notably nutritious, summertime meal. Such a refrigerator sends one shopping.

What usually happened to me, however, was that the fridge never got quite to that stage. Between it and the cabinets, I always imagined there was enough gump to turn out a respectable meal. I imagined this, of course, most keenly when it was late at night and the kids hadn't been fed. At such times the neighborhood takeout Chinese restaurant became Scylla to Colonel Sanders's Charybdis, and I became the Desperation Gourmet. The DG, if he shopped at all, grabbed a handful of stuff on his way to and from the subway and hoped to God the kids hadn't eaten the staples he remembered seeing in an obscure corner of the refrigerator only a few weeks ago.

I mean, is it really worthwhile going to the all-night greengrocer's for fresh dill when there's some in the crisper from this

Thursday? Or is it parsley in that plastic bag, and was it maybe *last* Thursday?

It's this sort of question that plagued the Desperation Gourmet as he wiggled his way around the N train in order to stand in front of a Chinese person who might get off at Canal Street. Tradition and inspiration were more useful to him in the kitchen than any recipes, but what he really needed was a photographic memory of its shelves.

About that can of tuna fish, for instance. Was it still there? Or did he feed it to the cats the last time he forgot to buy Tender Vittles? Certitude makes the difference between the tolerable and the wonderful. Tolerable, for instance, is spaghetti with lots of butter, fresh-grated cheese, and a couple of egg yolks. Plenty of protein and perfectly okay. Enjoyable is the same thing, only with an irregularly shaped pasta. But wonderful, especially when the wee bairns are muttering darkly about the wide range of options available to them through Family Court, requires that can of tuna. Which *always* turned out to have been either a figment of my imagination or to have become—just that afternoon—an after-school snack.

Short of a bright new padlock on the kitchen cabinets, there wasn't a great deal to be done about crazed snackers raiding the supplies (especially when their hunger was caused by the cook arriving home an hour or so late). But we decided that we could manage our inventory problem better if we shopped less casually.

We also told ourselves we would save money, and at least that part of the fantasy was true. So we pledged a New Beginning, which mostly means we agree on a week's worth of menus and make out a shopping list for a concerted swoop on the supermarket. We have two basic rules: Don't shop without a list, and don't buy anything that's not on it. Since divergence leads directly to bankruptcy, I tend to follow the rules. But I hate it.

When I say "hate," I ain't just whistlin' hyperbole. I shop for food the way some people shop for shoes or impressionist paintings. The quest itself is pleasurable. To wander from store to store—here considering the brightness of a bluefish's eyes, there discovering some baby eggplant—is my idea of a swell time. Even cruising the aisles of a supermarket can be a small adventure, and if I forget myself and add yet another jar of pimientos to the stock already in our pantry, so what? I am the master of my fate, I am the captain of my cart.

But when I carry a shopping list, it is the boss. My eyes move in circumscribed patterns; instead of being alive to new possibilities, they search specifics. That artistic pyramid of canned mackerel gives no pleasure; it's just another obstacle between me and the breadcrumbs. There is a difference between going for a walk in the woods and running desperately through the underbrush in order to catch a train, and though I'd like to stop and admire the way light filters through the tall pines, I can't. I am the list's errand boy, with aisles to go before I sleep.

I tell myself this is all nonsense. The list is not my enemy but my ally. When I follow it I save money. The list is For My Own Good. And the policeman is my friend.

Which, to be fair, he sometimes is. The Transit Authority cop who magically appears on the West 4th Street platform at three in the morning to stand between me and that group of large, drunken teen-agers is an okay fellow as far as I'm concerned— something I can certainly not say for the guy who ticketed me for speeding in Adams, New York, last summer. But the subway cop is there on his own hook. I didn't invent him (and you can bet I didn't invent the trooper upstate). When I use a shopping list, I actually create the instrument of my own oppression. To save a few pennies, I strangle my soul.

But we aren't talking about a few pennies here and there. We're talking dollars. And fives and tens. We are talking at least the $2.19 I spent on a quart of fresh-squeezed orange juice at a tony fruiterier last week. Probably about the sugar-snap peas instead of the green beans, too. And the walnut oil. But it was on special, so maybe it doesn't really count. I am sorry about the juice, though. That was really unforgivable. Also delicious.

You see what I mean? I'm alibi-ing the walnut oil away, sticking in a "probably"—where none belongs—about the sugar-snap peas, and remembering how good the orange juice tasted. If the juice had been only a little less backbreaking in price, I'd figure out some way to rationalize it, too.

But if it had been $1.50, or even a dollar, it would still have been a nonbudgeted item. A misdemeanor instead of a felony, perhaps, but a fiscal crime nonetheless. And one which, given the momentary presence of money in my pocket, I would gladly repeat.

And so, kicking and screaming all the while, I bind myself in chains of my own devising. Eyes on my scrap of paper, I march through the routine, crossing off items as they go into the cart, and buying only what the list allows. But as I stand in the checkout line, I am forced to admit that Rousseau was overly optimistic; without Hobbes, I'd have forgotten the garbage bags.

Actually, the list is more a Lockean compromise than hardcore Hobbes. It promises not mere survival but an orderly dinner, and up to a point, it delivers. But even without the constant worry about what—and with what—one is going to prepare for dinner, daily cooking can become onerous. Trying to cope with a teen-age audience that is at once ravenous and picky, one feels delight in cooking shade gradually into grudging surliness. Followed, one being a liberal, by guilt. One realizes that dinner is not a bad argument for the two-parent family.

And so, *Deo gratias*, does the other one. Which means that in addition to the discipline of the list, we began sharing kitchen duties; the Woman Warrior leapt into the breach of my discontent and took charge of cooking (*and* buying the catfood, toilet paper, etc.) on Mondays and Thursdays.

This started a couple of years ago, but much as I'd wanted it, the change made me nervous. Some of the initial unease had no doubt to do with my feeling I'd slid away from a domestic responsibility, but much of it was simple weirdness: I didn't like the idea of eating someone else's cooking. This was silly—I'm perfectly happy to be pampered at restaurants or at friends' homes—but I found it very hard to sit back and let someone cook *my* dinner in *my* kitchen. I chafed. I even cheated—going out to the kitchen under cover of seeking a glass of wine, I peered into the Woman Warrior's pots and critically smelled the cooking aromas. And if the food hadn't been good, the Pecksniff in me would shamelessly have second-guessed her.

Still, there have been compensating pleasures. For instance, hearing someone else's efforts get a "yecch" from the Tasteless Ones. Indeed, when this happened a few times, I found myself once again becoming the Woman Warrior's ally. I knew what it felt like to spend a lot of time working on a dinner only to be gonged before the pot had even reached the table. I sympathized.

I've also eaten well. The Woman Warrior, a healthnik manqué, has a totally different kitchen style from mine. She, for instance, has the patience to work with dried legumes and is rather fond of baking. I usually kamikaze my way in and out of the kitchen in a half hour, and I haven't baked anything more ambitious than baking-powder biscuits in years.

The realization that I was not only eating well, but also eating a broader range of meals than I would have ever got around to preparing by myself, set me thinking about the resistance I'd initially felt to being pushed out of the kitchen. (I know "pushed out of the kitchen" is hardly accurate, but allow me my illusions.) I thought back to days when I'd had a "real" job (allegedly nine to five, but far more often eight to eight) and had always shuffled assignments so that I got too much to do. This arrangement had the practical advantage of keeping me from getting bored and the neurotic one of giving me a built-in excuse for failing to do my best on any particular piece of the load. I suspect that my cooking often works the same way.

Sure, I can crank it up for the odd dinner party, but most workaday meals are a little on the flung-together side. Over the years I've developed a hundred or so serviceable main dishes— just good enough, in fact, to provide a lazy alternative on those rare days when I do have time to cook (see advantages, neurotic and practical, above).

I think it was probably some sort of response to the implicit challenge posed by the Woman Warrior's cooking (Q. Why do you describe this allegedly welcome assistance as a "challenge"? A: Shut up), to decide I should stretch out a little bit and go for A Big One. A Sunday afternoon about two months after the shift provided an opportunity, and the big one—complicated enough to be a two-person effort—was a vegetable chartreuse.

Despite the lurid name, no food coloring is involved; a chartreuse is a high-sided, circular baking dish. During much of that Sunday afternoon, when the ham was baking and the kids were lurching out from televised violence to ask when dinner was gonna be ready, the Woman Warrior and I labored over mounds of vegetables. We shelled peas, snapped beans, julienned carrots, cut cauliflower into florets, mashed potatoes, sliced squashes, separated cabbage leaves, trimmed Brussels sprouts, and had several spirited discussions. Finally, after parboiling each vegetable separately, we began to assemble the sculpture.

We lined the bottom and sides of the chartreuse with softened butter, and as I handed over the requisite veg, the Woman Warrior took them with trembling, buttery fingers and fit them neatly into place. Around the bottom of the pot, she arranged a single ring of peas (the butter keeps them from rolling), then filled in the circle with overlapping slices of zucchini and yellow squash. Along the sides—pressed into the butter and each one more or less standing on a pea—she placed alternating green beans and carrot sticks. After any offending ends sticking over the top were surgically removed, the bottom and sides were coated with about an inch or so of mashed potatoes. We lined the resulting pocket with cabbage leaves, filled them with a ring of sprouts and a centerpiece of cauliflower, doused this treasure trove with butter, then sealed it with more cabbage leaves. Finally we filled in the chartreuse with the remaining mashed potatoes and popped it into the oven, from which we'd just removed the ham.

Twenty minutes later, it was ready. As I finished carving the meat, the W.W. went kitchenward to invert and unmold the chartreuse. "Oh, look!" she cried delightedly. And then, somewhat dryly, "While there's still time."

We bounded into the kitchen to see it standing on its platter, a multicolored monument on a lake of butter. Then, as we watched with snakebit fascination, it began to move. Slowly—the Potato King later compared it to the films of flowers opening shown in his biology class—the mashed potatoes began to expand and sag. Under their pressure the beans and carrots dominoed outward, and the peas skied down the newly created slope. By the time we got it to the table, it looked like an outtake from *Close Encounters.*

It didn't taste bad, though, and the extra vegetables left over from the preparation made their way into a killer minestrone for the next night's dinner. The net result of one failure, one success, and one neurosis nudged slightly aside was not at all bad for a weekend's work.

But the critical breakthrough in the continuing cure of my kitchen neurosis resulted less from willpower than from the combined efforts of the Metropolitan Transit Authority, Mayor Koch, and the Transit Worker's Union. I suppose I should be grateful to them, but at the time of the subway strike, gratitude was not much in my mind. Among other and considerably more dramatic effects, the strike played hell with the dinner hour.

By a series of compromises (if I had my druthers, I'd eat sometime between nine and ten, drink myself into a pleasant drowsiness, and stumble from the table to bed), we had an officially stated policy of dinner at seven, which meant that we usually managed to get food on the table by seven-thirty. Much later than that, we caught a good deal of grief from the Surly Ones. Earlier never happened.

Enter the transit strike. Exit the good ol' D train, farewell the quirky QB. Disaster. For reasons of his own, my employer provided me with a car for the duration, but this turned out to be a mixed blessing. Given the nightly reenactment of the tortures of the damned held at the mouth of the Brooklyn-Battery Tunnel, it was foolish for me even to think about leaving Manhattan until seven-thirty or so. Which meant I never got home until eight-thirty. Which meant dinner at nine-thirty. Which further meant that the kids were grumpy and yelled at me when I walked in the door. Which was a big mistake, let me tell you, because after a slalom down the Prospect Expressway, I was in no mood for criticism. I became, I blush to admit, short of temper. The spots from when I threw a cup of coffee at my firstborn faded after three months, but it would have served me right if I'd had to repaper.

We were saved from permanent transformation into a nest of snarling dogs when the Woman Warrior announced that she was taking over the kitchen, schedule or no. Since I had to leave for the city at five-thirty every morning in order to beat the traffic, she did all the shopping as well (not all that much of a hardship; she actually *likes* making lists). Oddly enough, she partnered herself with the dreaded Pierre Franey, who had by then collected a heap of his newspaper columns into a book; turns out that if you shop with the specific recipes in mind, it's pretty useful. So I would telephone as I left the office, and dinner appeared not at some indefinite period after I arrived, but virtually as I walked in the door. That it was there at all was a blessing; that it was good, a miracle. Especially because much of the cooking was accomplished while the Youngest Member was exploring the world, an erratic phenomenon that often turned the Woman Warrior into the one-armed, one-hour gourmet, which is a handicap Franey hadn't imagined.

The long-term effect of all this is that the kitchen now seems to be less *mine* than *ours*, and we trade dinner duty not on any preordained schedule but according to who's got more time. But I hasten to add, however, that something approaching a formal nightly dinner remains a necessity. After all, if transit workers could cure *every* neurosis, they'd be earning so much money they'd never have to go on strike.

TUNA SAUCE FOR SPAGHETTI

After putting the pasta in boiling water, cover the bottom of a heavy frying pan with about ¼ inch olive oil. Set heat at medium, and as oil gets hot, mince 2 large cloves garlic and add them to the pan. As soon as the garlic has begun to turn brown, add 1 undrained can of oil-packed tuna and stir it vigorously through the hot oil. It should be broken into fairly tiny fragments by the time you're through. Add several sprinklings of dried oregano, a few twists from the pepper grinder, and—just before you pour the sauce over the spaghetti—1 tablespoon or so of butter. Freshly grated Parmesan is a nice, though not absolutely necessary, accompaniment.

SUMMER VEGETABLE SAUTÉ

Hobbes would probably solve the culinary war of each against all by reducing everything to a stew; Rousseau, wishing to leave the state of nature untouched, would push salads. This crisp sauté of seasonal vegetables, a fine accompaniment for whatever piece of meat or fish is coming off the charcoal grill, is a Lockean compromise that serves four. It is also quick to make.

1. Peel and slice 1 large yellow onion and sauté it in a half-stick butter over very low heat, stirring from time to time to prevent scorching.

2. Scrape (if necessary) a half-bunch of carrots, cutting them into thumb-sized length. Quarter the thick ends, halve the medium-sized chunks, and cook the pieces, covered, in boiling salted water for 3 to 4 minutes. Drain, rinse thoroughly with cold water, and reserve.

3. Cut 4 small zucchini into pieces the same size as the carrots, and when the onion has turned golden, add them to the sauté pan. Stir to coat them thoroughly in butter and increase heat to

medium high. Cook for about 2 minutes, turning occasionally.

4. Add the reserved carrots to the pan, salt to taste, and sprinkle generously with tarragon (author's choice), dill (Woman Warrior's favorite), or thyme (universally acceptable alternative). Serve as soon as the carrots are heated through, about 3 minutes.

———

SCOTCH BROTH

Given a couple of pounds of lamb and a few vegetables, I'd probably cube the lamb, dredge it in flour, then brown it in a heavy skillet. When it was brown, I'd add equal parts red wine and water to cover, season it with minced garlic and rosemary, cover it, and let it bubble for a while. The vegetables would get cooked separately, and—once the sauce on the lamb had thickened—I'd serve the meat over noodles, with the vegetables on the side. The Woman Warrior, however, would be tempted to prepare what some might call Scotch broth, but what she calls "How to Stuff Brats with Turnips" soup.

1. Put the meat, in one piece, into a heavy pot with about 1 cup each chopped carrots, turnips, and leeks. Add 3 to 4 tablespoons barley and an equal amount of parboiled split peas. Cover with 2 qts. water, add salt and pepper, and bring to a boil. Skim off any foam, if necessary; then cover the pot, and let simmer for at least 3 hours, checking every now and then to make sure no more water is needed.

2. Shut off the heat and remove the meat. Let it stand for a few minutes to firm up, then cut it into bite-sized chunks. While it's standing, skim and discard as much fat as possible off the top of the liquid. Return the chunked meat to the pot, together with 2 generous handfuls carefully rinsed chopped kale (or spinach). As soon as the soup has returned to a rolling boil, stir in 1 generous handful of chopped parsley, and serve immediately.

First, Catch
Your Refrigerator

*F*rom time to time—prompted now by ecological consciousness, then by short-tempered communications from Con Ed—I fantasize living without electricity. Mostly I think it would be good for me. You know, up with the sun, to bed at nightfall, hey bop bop, livin' off the land.

Fortunately, these fantasies have never been realized for longer than it takes the power company to get itself straightened out after a hurricane, for I battle off urges toward the simple life by means of counterfantasies. I think, for instance, of never having seen Luis Tiant's commercial for Colonial Bacon and realize that I'd be the poorer for it. Ditto hearing Vin Scelsa.

Oddly, given my predilection for things culinary, kitchen appliances have never proved particularly useful defensive weapons. Sure, I'd miss the electric juicer, but I'd be getting all my sunshine vitamins from the original source. And you can always toast your English muffins in the oven.

Alert readers will notice that I haven't mentioned the refrigerator. I am not alone in this; nobody ever talks about refrigerators. It's not that they're unseemly—a sort of herpes simplex of the appliance world—but that they're taken for granted. Consider the "Apartments" classifieds: They hype many an electric goody—your AC, your dw, your W/D—but when was the last time you saw someone trying to rent an apartment on the basis of its marvelous refrigerator? This is patently unfair, for lemme tell you, you can get by quite handily without an air conditioner, a dishwasher, or a washer/dryer combo. Easy. But you can't get by without a fridge. Ask the man who doesn't own one.

Our plunge into the twilight world of the refrigeratorless coincided with our recent removal to Flatbush. Where, having forked over a sum of money that would have kept us in dinners at Lutèce for a good long time, we became proud owners of a house (actually, we're the shell-shocked possessors of a mortgage, but that's another story). Said house has everything you could reasonably want, including a large and airy kitchen; on its floor, there's a handsome mark where once a refrigerator stood.

Noticing almost immediately that it was gone—we're a pretty observant bunch—we set out to buy another one. Which is not as easy as you might think. To the untrained eye, all refrigerators this side of certain 1940s models in the mode of the Chrysler building look pretty much alike. But to the potential buyer, the refrigerator universe is infinite in its variety. They come side-by-side or top and bottom; white or colored in—oh mysterious term—"decorator" colors; frost-free and conventional; left-handed and right-handed; and nobody's got the model you finally decide on anyway—except for one guy who thinks he can deliver it a week from Tuesday.

Meanwhile, life goes on. The sun, in its ecological purity, rises and sets, and you are forced either into drinking the morning coffee black or (shudder) actually going outside and buying milk before that first desperate cup goes down.

We have been, as they say, making do. We started out with a thermos bottle to hold coffee milk overnight, but—after the second day when a half stick of butter had reduced itself to a greasy smear—graduated to a Styrofoam cooler. This little number works just fine, provided, of course, that one of us feeds it ice cubes. To be sitting there in the late afternoon—afraid to leave because the men with the real refrigerators are going to be along any minute (you bet)—and feel the water in the cooler growing relentlessly more tepid is to spend the day in Harry Hope's saloon.

But even when the icemaid cometh, problems remain. Suitably packed with ice, the cooler keeps stuff cold, but so packed, there's room for only a milk carton, a soda can or two, some butter, and maybe the odd half-lemon or lump of cream cheese. This forces a fundamental redefinition of the leftover problem from "Leftovers: How to Use" to "Leftovers: How to Avoid." Roasts and casseroles are out, under the new dispensation, and God's own portion control is in. Chops are particularly helpful in this regard; everybody gets one, and that's it. It's so simple it feels almost as pure as living without electricity.

UNLEFT VEAL CHOPS

For 4 chops (and 4 people, right?), crush 3 large cloves garlic, and blend with ½ tablespoon dried oregano. Brush each side of the ¾-inch veal chops with walnut oil and sort of smear/press the oregano and garlic mixture into them. Broil, either indoors or out, only until the chops are warm in the center. Serve with lemon wedges.

Yesterday's News

I am, I like to think, a pretty elegant fellow. As delusions go, this is not as dangerous as believing I can lick any man in the house, but it does have its drawbacks. For instance last week, when I should have been home defending my basement against the spring rains, I was out shopping for cloth napkins. Mostly, that was because of the napkin rings, which I'll get to later, but it was also because I have this problem with paper napkins. It is called a mustache.

I like cloth napkins, not simply because I desire to live in the manner of publishers and bankers, but because my vaunted elegance does not prevent pieces of egg salad from building nests on my upper lip. Hudson's Mr. Big's are okay for wiping away the occasional stray, but during a hard-core attack of spareribs, paper napkins are simply not up to the job. If anything, they are counterproductive; they fray, and instead of being grease-spattered, I become festooned with tatters of pastel paper, which is not attractive.

Anyway, cloth napkins are cheaper in the long run. This sounds like Blondie ("Guess how much money I saved by buying this new hat, Dagwood?"), but it's true. At least I think it is, which is good enough. There's an initial capital outlay, but after that you're home free; buying paper napkins is like being nibbled to death by ducks. Maintenance? With two teen-age men and a four-month-old woman in the house, the washing machine never stops anyway. Toss a couple of napkins in, who knows the difference? And you don't need to iron them anymore, because they're permanent press (let's hear it for petroleum by-products, folks).

Still, there are difficulties with cloth napkins. The very quality that makes them economically defensible—their durability—carries with it some risks. I mean, when you're pushing the cart up the paper-product aisle at Food City, the choice between Marcal and Scot's doesn't paralyze you. But buying napkins with which you are going to have a meaningful relationship for a number of years forces you into an orgy of self-criticism.

Alert readers will notice how cleverly I've segued into the second person. I used to try the same trick when I was in therapy, and it didn't fool anyone then, either. What I mean is, I found buying cloth napkins an alarmingly revelatory experience.

Lace, for instance, was out. The cognitive dissonance between lace and a tuna-noodle casserole is more than I could bear. We would constantly be blowing the food budget in a desperate attempt to live up to our napkins.

Ditto the various designer creations. They are as sleek as Ferraris—some have what appear to be racing stripes—and would instantly transform the dining-room table from the antique we pretend it to be into the used furniture it is. Also, I'm not sure I want to wipe my mouth on a machine.

Speaking of which, there is such a thing as too much petroleum by-product. The one hundred percent polyester napkins that I saw would certainly never require ironing, but they are—in their perpetually stain-resistant splendor—a genuinely lunatic creation. I *want* my napkins to absorb food. Otherwise I could just wipe my face with some nice waxed paper and be done with it.

But the range of choice in the cotton/polyester group was still staggering. Prints, from gingham checks to art nouveau that would make Aubrey Beardsley blush, and colors for which there are no names. (That is not quite true; it's just that the names are beyond me. I'm okay on red-orange-yellow-green-blue-indigo-violet, but if someone asked me about mauve or puce, I would stammer helplessly. And now that you mention it, I was never too sure about indigo.) Anyway, I grabbed some napkins that are either mauve or puce, I think, and fled. We've been using them for about a week now, and they're real nice.

But why, you ask, if I am so passionate about the subject of cloth napkins, have I been making do with paper for the last several years. Well, mostly because we didn't have napkin rings, and if you think I'm going to risk wiping my mouth with something that's been near the kids, you're as loony as a polyester napkin. But when I was looking around for the perfect anniversary present for the Woman Warrior, I came across a pair of hand-worked eighteenth-century silver napkin rings that would knock your eyes out. Once we had those in the house, I could go ahead and buy cloth napkins and save a lot of money. Er . . . maybe I should get Blondie in here to explain this.

―――――――

CHICKEN VERONIQUE

Preheat oven to 200 degrees. Split 4 chicken breasts, and sauté them, in two batches, over medium-high heat in a scant half-stick of butter and a little bit of vegetable or peanut oil. As the pieces are done, put them on a serving platter in the oven.

When the last piece of chicken is cooked, turn off the pan and let it cool slightly. Add to it 2 tablespoons finely chopped shallots and stir. When the shallots wilt, turn the heat back on high and immediately add 1 glass dry white wine. As the wine boils, stir up the brown bits from the bottom of the frying pan.

When the wine is reduced by about half, lower the heat and add 1 cup heavy cream and 1 cup fresh seedless grapes, from which you've pulled the stems. Salt—generously, the grapes are sweet—and pepper. Stir occasionally until the sauce thickens (about 5 minutes). Add a couple of tablespoons chopped parsley and pour over the chicken pieces. Serve immediately.

White rice is the perfect accompaniment; fine noodles are okay. In either case, if we ate like this all the time, I'd have bought lace. Serves 4.

Not By Bread Alone

The toaster's broken. Not in a flamboyant way, which would cause us to admit defeat and chuck it, but only in the pop-up department. Instead of knowing that the toast is done when we hear it, we know it's burned when we smell it. This is not efficient.

Toast consumption has remained constant, but bread usage has soared. Every other day, in a vain attempt to anticipate the sanitation department's whimsies, we lug out garbage bags loaded with hunks of bread-shaped charcoal. In this way, we do our bit for the inflationary spiral. Our repetitive toastings also, I suspect, gladden hearts at Con Ed. You would think we'd either get the damn thing fixed or buy another.

But we won't. At any rate, we haven't. Our economic logic is the reverse of the scofflaws'. Rather than absorb a relatively small expense in the present, they sit around and wait for the computer to nail them with penalty charges and interest; we seem willing to take an endless series of present small losses in order to avoid buying a new appliance. I dunno about people with parking tickets (I think they're wrong, although the computer just might slip up and let them slide through), but we're crazy. Given the price of decent bread, we could amortize a toaster in a month.

Maybe our fundamental problem is we don't take toast seriously enough. If so—and I don't want to sound like a bleeding-heart liberal—we're victims of society. Toast is the afterthought of the breakfast special (served six to eleven a.m.), the last resort of forgetful parents ("We're out of raisin bran again? How about a nice piece of toast?"), or just the stuff that holds sandwiches together. It's about as glamorous as a bath mat. On the other hand, who wants to leave a steaming shower and stand on a cold tile floor? Toast is important. Toast is the Real Stuff. It was zwieback when we were teething, and is manna when we're seeing the light at the end of the flu.

But toast isn't just for babes, convalescents, and dowager duchesses. Toast—even white toast, in its unassuming way—can be special. Think of coming in from the snow to hot cocoa and cinnamon toast. Think, too, of Western cuisine's answer to the Orient's subtle delight in contrasting textures, our wonderful combinations of cold and hot.

And not just the morning marmalade, either. But smoked salmon, with chopped onion, capers, and coarse black pepper. Bagels and lox were never like this.

Think of pâté, of a thin layer of steak tartare, or even—damn the expense—of caviar. Nothing is too good for toast. It deserves the very best we can lavish on it. It is crisp, it is warm, it is buttery, it is faithful. . . .

Maybe I'll get the kids a toaster for Christmas. They gave me a football once.

Seduced and Unabandoned

Amonth or so after we'd moved to our current residence, Anna disappeared. She came back, I must say, looking suspiciously sleek and well-fed. Not for her the life of an alley cat; she'd obviously charmed some stranger into pampering her. But she tore herself away from the delights of canned food and returned home to Moist Meals and us.

She'd been gone for a full week when the Mad Baker, on his way to school one morning, spotted her lounging beneath a parked car. "Anna?" he said. She emerged and deigned to be picked up. He carried her home, where there ensued a regular orgy of laughter and purring.

I participated. Though I'm theoretically not fond of cats— there are three in the house, none of which belongs to me—I make an exception in Anna's case. Some years ago, when I was first falling in love with her mistress, Anna captured me *en passant*. Linked by our belief that the Woman Warrior was pretty swell, we gradually overcame our mutual suspicions, settling first into grudging respect, then affection.

Anna tested me, though. She had been a farm cat during the Woman Warrior's hippie-dippy-livin'-off-the-land days and had made few concessions to apartment life. Oh, sure, it was nice to know there was a cat box and some cuddling to come home to, but real life began on the fire escape that led to the tangled, urban back yard. The door to freedom was on my side of the bed, and whenever she wanted in or out, she came to me. A sharp nip on my toes meant, "Open the door, buster, I've got things to do"; a remarkable symphony of bangings and scratchings meant, "Wake up and let me in, stupid. Don't you know it's *cold* out here?" If Sandburg had lived with Anna, he would have thought twice about that metaphor.

But I forgave Anna—my astonished joy at being in that bed was so great that the inconvenience of rising from it during the night was as nothing—and after a while she began bringing me presents. Mice, mostly. And once, a bat. I think her intentions were good (I mean, she probably wouldn't think it was all that great if I gave her a book).

So when she disappeared from our new house, I missed her and worried about her. But not as badly as the Woman Warrior did. I was—am, really—an interloper in their relationship; once, when we were packing to move here and got caught up in one of those nasty fights that seem inevitably to accompany moving, Anna came between us, leapt up in the Woman Warrior's arms, and began licking at her face to groom and comfort her. It's no wonder that her mistress grieved all the time Anna was gone.

There were bad dreams at night, worse fantasies during the day. The subway runs near our house; we pondered the third rail. Or perhaps, given the noise of passing trains, Anna had failed to hear an oncoming car as she crossed the street. Or worse yet, maybe she'd felt evicted by our about-to-be-born baby: "She kept trying to curl up in my lap," said the Woman Warrior, "but there wasn't any lap *left*."

Or maybe, spritelike, she'd just moved on. "She came to me at a bad time," went the mystically optimistic recollection, "and stayed through some that were worse. Maybe now that things are all right, she's helping someone else out. It's just the sort of thing she'd do."

The problem with this rationalization, to the extent we'd

managed to make ourselves believe it, is that Anna's return became virtually a guarantee of rough times ahead. But for a cat, she's not bad.

Besides, the only relationships that don't have bad times are exceedingly short. We didn't need Anna to guarantee such periods; we built in our own—not so much when we fell in love as when we decided to do something about it. Late in the spring after Anna's return, for instance, I found myself wandering around the back yard in a severe mope. The stumpy little bushes that were naked when we'd moved in had decided to cover themselves in brilliant red flowers, but I was dying.

Not any faster than I'd been in cocoa season, mind you, but dying nonetheless. As God's own salad days were going on around me, I was celebrating—in the loosest sense of the word—my fortieth birthday. Inescapably middle-aged (now, indeed, lurching toward my forty-first), I braced for the mid-life crazies.

I'm actually kind of interested in them. Back in the days when everybody was having nervous breakdowns, I was never able to fit one in. When the car carrying a gabbling, drooling acid casualty arrived at Bellevue's emergency room, I was always behind the wheel. Later on I would visit my friends, whisked away to more pleasant institutions by family money, and envy them their eerie serenity. One woman, a bundle of tightly wound nervous energy during countless neighborhood struggles, was professionally unraveled at a large stone mansion overlooking the mid-Hudson. The May I turned thirty, we played a desultory croquet game on its lawn. The sunlight sparkled on the river, and I reminded her whenever her turn came up. She was, she said, thinking, and her eyes did not sparkle at all.

I went back to saving the world, which occupation I was then practicing by fooling around with columns of numbers until they added up in some unexpected way, and she went to California. Occasionally we wrote, purposes that crossed in the mail. I was pleased when my figures added up to more sanitation trucks;

she was delighted when hers became a new self. Somehow, it seems, she graduated from addition to multiplication, joined Arica, and became a decade. It is over now, I hope.

You see what I mean about the mid-life crazies. There we were, you and I, starting off on the usual romp through the world of family life and bad puns, and the next thing you know, I'm carrying on like the Ancient Mariner. I'm really sorry about that. It just sort of happened. I was, I thought, thinking.

But I was only remembering, which is different. Also more dangerous, for it leads one to behave thoughtlessly. I spent the morning after my fortieth birthday attempting to explain this distinction to the Youngest Member, who comforted me with her favorite noise. It is phonemically indistinguishable from a Bronx cheer, but it's the thought that counts.

That, at least, is what my mother always told me on those occasions when I ripped open birthday presents and found pajamas, and you would think I'd have learned it by now. But no. On my today-I-am-a-middle-aged-man birthday, I opened a gift from the Woman Warrior and launched a vicious attack on it. It was, I announced, ugly, cheap, tawdry, and looked as if it had come from a subway discount shop.

It was none of those things, and I apparently was complaining that it had failed to stop me from being forty, but the words kept spewing out. The boys, sitting at the table and watching their father foam at the mouth, were horrified, and the Woman Warrior hurt. Soon, the special bottle of birthday wine still unfinished, they left me at the table alone with my shame.

I've done it again, haven't I? Snuck off and gotten all melancholy on you. Again, I'm sorry. But only the Youngest Member is entitled to her *tabula rasa*; on me, it would look silly as a sunsuit.

Which is not to say that I'm forbidden fantasies. In some ways, they are an occupational hazard; journalists spend an undue amount of time covering the rich and powerful, and the illusion that we actually belong among them is seductive. During one presidential campaign, for instance, I ate two thousand-dollar-a-plate dinners, a five-hundred-dollar breakfast, and a hundred-dollar box lunch on a five-day sprint through New England. And novelists are *supposed* to spend their working hours in fantasyland. Finally, of course, there are occasional plum assignments.

Back when I was a stripling lad of thirty-eight, I was preparing for my annual post-Christmas slump when fate—in the altogether pleasing form of the Woman Warrior—intervened with a question: "How would you like to go to Paris for a couple of weeks to eat, all expenses paid, in a series of great restaurants?" She'd been assigned by a travel magazine to do precisely that and wanted to bring at least one of the comforts of home along with her. Since Anna speaks no French, she picked me.

I thought I was a fine choice myself and promptly—hers was really not the sort of question that requires a whole lot of consideration—signed on. So we made arrangements for the care and feeding of the kids (who speak French but eat mostly pizza and potatoes) and took off.

It was wonderful.

Oysters, for instance. Belons, Claires, Portugaises . . . crunchily batter-fried; roasted, with pernod, *comme façon* gourmet; in a sorrel-scented soup; and raw at an endless succession of streetside vendors.

And sauces that would break your heart. The one, single, absolutely perfect hollandaise bathing an equally perfect poached turbot; a mousseline, bejeweled with capers and green peppercorns, over grilled raie; a lemon-sharp reduction of tomatoes on a crisp, moist feuillite of sole. . . .

The hits just kept on coming; the misses—once-excellent restaurants living off their history—were amazingly few. Late one Sunday afternoon, for instance, as we slogged through the mud and joggers of the Bois de Boulogne, we realized we'd become ravenously hungry. There being no suitably historic restaurant nearby, we decided we'd eat at the first place we found when we left the park. This turned out to be the Pavillon des Princes, whose main entrance—a tribute to the various uses of Formica—

looked disconcertingly like an International House of Pancakes. "This," said the Woman Warrior, "is *tacky*."

True enough, but it was the only restaurant in sight, and we were *very* hungry. In the outer room, with its post-Truman factory architecture, a few families were recovering from their Sunday dinners and quarreling amiably over Calvados and Armagnac; the captain took us past them, into a bar that had clearly met the needs of generations of thirsty French, and sat us at a scarred wooden table. He brought us a bottle of Beaujolais *primeur*—the soft, fragile wine that survives for only a few months past October's harvest—some fine, crusty rolls, and a pot of Normandy butter. We sipped, we nibbled, we warmed ourselves—and we decided this might not be so bad after all. Then he came over and told us the kitchen was closed.

"Not even, perhaps, some soup?" quavered the Woman Warrior. He regretted, but no. Then, perhaps touched by our pitiable condition, he allowed as how they might be able to rustle up a few cold things. Some *salade du crabe*, perhaps, and a bit of *jambon de pays*. Would this please *m'sieu-dame?*

Oh, it would, it would. The plates arrived, beautifully arranged, a mountain of fresh flaky crab, flanked by eggs, tomato, and a lightly bound mélange of peas, potato, and carrot. On the side a mustardy mayonnaise so good we used it on the ham as well, a stone jar of cornichons, and more rolls. And more wine. We began, at one point, to laugh in the delighted way of very young children at a birthday party.

And then the tarts. A bottom layer of *pâté brisée* miraculously crisp under its rich plateau of soft custard and poached fruit—apricots for madame, mirabelles for me. A little coffee to warm us, needlessly, against the mist, and we were on the way home.

Outside, with slightly drunken enthusiasm, we marched several blocks in the wrong direction and found ourselves lost in a maze of suburban streets. After a serious consult with her ever-present pocket guide to Paris, the Woman Warrior announced that we'd fallen off the edge of the map.

And perhaps we had. Maybe we were in Oz, or the other side of the looking glass. Or perhaps just in Paris, and love. Ah . . . but you shouldn't get the impression that our domestic life is made up of alternate scenes from Erich Segal and Sam Peckinpah. Mostly, rather like the tarts, we enjoy a comfortable plateau. For instance, we haven't done anything dramatic on a Wednesday for *months*.

Wednesday, you see, is marketing day. Not the fun part of shopping, but the grim detergent-and-catfood-and-paper-towel-and-disposable-diaper trek through the local supermarket. This disagreeable task—which I bear with considerable grace, if anyone should ask you—is preceded by the making of lists, which is in turn preceded by the creation of the week's menus. There is a certain amount of intramural hauling and tugging during these negotiations, but there's real pleasure in the imaginary creation of seven dinners at a shot.

Also occasional contretemps, as in:

SPOUSE A: How about I do a chicken scarpariello on Thursday?

SPOUSE B: Do you have to? I'm really tired of it.

SPOUSE A: How "tired"? I haven't made it in . . . I don't think *ever*.

SPOUSE B: I know *you* haven't, but I make it all the time.

SPOUSE A: You never made it for *me*.

And so on.

Awkward as such moments may be—and they aren't *that* terrible; in another thirty-five or forty years we'll probably outgrow such petty jealousies—they fade as stars before the sunrise when compared with our running differences over The Big Picture. Mostly, there is this question about meat.

My own position can best be indicated by a bit of history. Back in the days when I was first wrestling with the printed word, I was given a children's missal to use at Sunday Mass. The priest and altar boys whipped along in muttered Latin as I tried to keep pace with them in my beginner's English. This represented enough of a technical struggle that I probably didn't get as much praying done as would have been good for me, but I still recall my delight when I came across a passage reading, "It is meet and just . . ." For an embarrassingly long time, I regarded this weekly ritual as an expression of gratitude to God for making roast beef, and it was one of the Mysteries of the Faith—a joyful one, to be sure—that I entered into most heartily.

Not so the Woman Warrior. Meatwise, she doesn't actually play the role of the Antichrist, but she can take your ordinary steak or leave it alone. Indeed, she is so good at leaving it that she was for a number of years a vegetarian, and you might imagine that our different tastes would from time to time create a little tension. If so, you would be right.

But reaching a theoretical compromise has been surprisingly easy. For reasons aesthetic, medical, and economic, we try to do two or three meatless meals a week. Not only is this no hardship—the Woman Warrior has a nifty repertoire of vegetarian dishes—but it's been a chance for me to muck around with some new modes of cooking. (I notice by the way she recently larrupped through a lamb stew that our carnivorous nights are not what you'd call an intolerable burden on the Woman Warrior either.)

Still, goodwill is not always enough. We were, last Wednesday morning, sitting on the bed surrounded by cookbooks and cats when we confronted a crisis. Consider this weekly lineup:

WED: Omelettes w lox and cream cheese
THURS: Chicken sautéed w rosemary and garlic
FRI: Scottish bread soup
SAT: ???
SUN: Braised smoked ham w tarragon cream
MON: Pasta w cauliflower sauce
TUES: Eggs Benedict

To me, the vacant spot on Saturday cried out for red meat. Only two nights of the six—Thursday and Sunday—were what I considered meat meals (if it wasn't an egg dish, they'd call it Ham Benedict). Anna, unambiguously carnivorous, didn't disagree, but to the Woman Warrior only Monday qualified as meatless. Eggs Benedict are *obviously* meat, the bread soup is made with beef stock, and, "Fish, fowl, and meat are dietetically the same."

Dietetically, maybe; spiritually, no. I was willing to give in on the Eggs Benedict (I can always slide a couple extra pieces of ham into mine), but held firm on the bread soup. Meat is not a liquid.

On the other hand, the stock in question is not your College Inn Beef Broth. It is a loving distillation of some splendid shinbones given us by our butcher and is practically the essence of marrow. If pushed to the wall, I was going to have a hard time defending it. Deciding that a tactical retreat might be preferable to a rout, I offered some dire warnings about the inevitable onset of *gouamba* and agreed to cheese blintzes.

Then I bit her on the thigh.

***

FRENCH FRIED POTATOES

To celebrate Anna's return, we declared a holiday from budgeting and feasted. The Mad Baker got to pick the menu and brought the fatted-calf metaphor up to date by decreeing steak, french fries, and chocolate cake. Asked to suggest a green vegetable that wouldn't actually ruin his dinner, he permitted frozen peas. But the french fries were, at his command, real.

Spoiled by too many hasty luncheonette meals, I'd forgotten how good real french fries can be. They're a bit of a drag to make, but they exist on a different plane of reality than any of the curious prefab versions. There are two ways to cook them: the first version is merely wonderful, the second, fall-on-the-floor delicious.

Easy: Wash and peel 1 large, firm, potato per person; cut them into strips no more than ½-inch wide, and put them in a bowl of cool, salted water. After about a half-hour, drain them thoroughly, and cook them—without crowding—in fat at 365 degrees. Using a heavy cast-iron frying pan, you should be able to do about one potato at a time. When they're done—about 5 minutes, which you can judge by color—salt them and let them drain onto paper towels. The first ones can keep warm in a 200-degree oven while the later batches are cooking.

Fancier: Cook them in two stages, the first, at about 320 degrees, just until they stop bubbling (about 2 minutes); the second, after allowing them to drain and dry for at least 5 minutes, at 365 degrees until they crisp (another 2 to 3 minutes).

~~~~~~~~~~

COLD BEEF VINAIGRETTE

Life may not begin at forty, but it goes on. Though we have none of us forgotten that birthday dinner, the people who love me have forgiven me and are hungry again. But it is too hot to cook. But salads aren't a real dinner, and besides, the interesting ones are yucky. The Muscular Lads crave meat. This dish cold/hot in the manner of Szechuan Hacked Chicken, satisfies.

1. For 4 people cut about 1½ lbs. very rare roast beef as thin as possible (good quality deli meat is fine if you don't have any leftovers). Shred the slices into strips and put them in a bowl with 2 large red onions, halved and sliced thin.

2. Cover with a dressing of 6 oz. olive oil, 1 oz. red wine vinegar, 1 tablespoon prepared Dijon mustard, a few mashed anchovies (I like to use 8 or 10 filets), and several shakes of dried red pepper. Mix thoroughly, cover, and refrigerate for at least 4 hours.

3. One hour before serving, remove the salad, stir again, and add a couple of tablespoons of chopped fresh parsley (or dill). Stir again a few times before serving, ideally with good French or Italian bread.

CHEESE BLINTZES

We use a slightly heavier than usual crepe batter for the outsides, and because we usually make these in quantity, we don't sauté the completed blintzes, but drizzle butter over them and bake them at 425 degrees in a buttered baking dish until they crisp up (about 15 minutes). To fill a dozen blintzes, mix together 1¼ lbs. farmer's cheese (or hoop cheese if you can find it), 2 large eggs, the juice of half a lemon, a pinch of salt, 2 generous tablespoons sugar, and several gratings fresh nutmeg. Put a goodly daub of the mixture into the center of each crepe, fold them into envelopes, and cook. That's all, folks.

Kitchen Cabinet
Considers Budget

We have books. We have sheet upon sheet of graph paper and lots of tiny bits of cardboard labeled things like "sink" and "d/w." We have a vision of a new kitchen. Basically, we want the kitchen to *feel* as old as the rest of the house, but to function with the efficiency and cleanliness of a first-class surgery.

Right now, it does neither. The kitchen appears to have been "modernized" about thirty years ago—a dating we arrive at by the fact that the inoperative dishwasher proudly bears chrome lettering identifying it as an "Electric Sink." Actually, to call it inoperative is to mislead; the bits of food that make their way down through its aging rubber gasket and into its pit allow our Electric Sink to function as a singularly efficient roach condo, which makes it more a child of nature than you would want your dishwasher to be.

And then there is the stove.

Or perhaps there is the floor; I'm not sure which is responsible. The point is that the stove tilts forward at an alarming angle. And by alarming I don't mean simply that the olive oil in which you are attempting to brown onions races toward one side of the sauté pan, but that failure to arrange said pan with geometric precision means that the whole damn thing may skid to the floor and permanently disfigure your infant daughter who is crawling around beneath it.

Which is among the least of the stove's problems. Though age has not staled its infinite variety, time has chewed the bejeezus out of its insulation. Turn on the oven and the porcelainized enamel surface above it becomes an instant hot plate. This is actually handy for keeping bacon warm, and for melting butter, but makes keeping a constant oven temperature something of an adventure. Particularly because you often have to open the oven to slide a knife inside the edge of the door beside it to get out a pot or pan because the handle snapped off the storage door a couple of months ago. And by the way, if the knife you're planning to use has been resting on the stove top for a while, you'd better have remembered your potholders.

Too late, huh? Okay, over to the sink to run cold water on the burn. Not so fast. Watch out for that treacherous seam where the linoleum started to buckle weirdly after the flood from the faulty bathtub drain upstairs. And don't bother trying to turn the cold water handle either. Reach with your remaining hand for the screwdriver that certainly ought to be around here somewhere and turn the screw in the top of the tap counterclockwise. There now, that's better, isn't it.

You will notice that I haven't mentioned counter space. There is a reason. Except for the glass roof of the roach condo and the hot, tilty part of the stove above the oven, there's a total of twelve inches of counter space. Occupied, in seeming perpetuity, by the dish drainer.

Still, what the kitchen lacks in counters, it makes up for in doors. It has five of them (a phenomenon perhaps not unrelated to the paucity of work space). One leads to the cellar, one to the living room, another to the pantry, the fourth to the back yard, and the last to (are you ready for this?) the butler's pantry. That's a lot of doors. I suppose they were useful for the comings and goings of the servants. We do not have servants.

Indeed, judging from the truly terrifying estimates brought to us by serious-minded contractors, we don't have enough money to redo the kitchen. But we plan, and scheme, and gradually our relationship with the kitchen takes on the depressing overtones of a marriage where one partner is secretly considering a divorce. We dream, but we make do.

Meanwhile, we've decided to stay together for the sake of the children. Who presumably would prefer dinner every night to a level floor.

GRANDMAMA'S TORTELLINI
(*requires no oven*)

2 lbs. frozen tortellini
1½ cups heavy cream
2 lbs. peas (in pods) or one 10-ounce
    frozen package
6 tablespoons fresh-grated Parmesan
½ lb. prosciutto
1 tablespoon butter
Salt, pepper, olive oil

1. Put a large pot of water for the pasta on to boil. Salt it, add about 1 tablespoon olive oil. As the water heats, bring the cream quickly to a boil, then reduce heat to a bare simmer.

2. When the pasta water boils, add the tortellini, and cook according to package directions (about 15 minutes). Prepare the peas as usual.

3. Cream the butter and half the Parmesan together, divide into 5 or 6 clumps, add—one at a time—to cream, stirring after each addition.

4. Chop the prosciutto coarsely, brown in a medium-hot frying pan until crisp. Drain and reserve.

5. As soon as tortellini is tender, drain it and mix quickly with the prosciutto, drained peas, and a few generous twists of black pepper. Mix thoroughly, taste for salt, and serve with additional cheese on side. Serves 6.

Upstairs, Downstairs

*B*ecause post office policy seems recently to have shifted from sloth to whimsicality, one could more accurately say that *The New Yorker* hadn't arrived yet than complain that it was late. In either case, on a day when the magazine's appearance could almost have been expected, it didn't come. Also, the Youngest Member extended my reading time by taking a longer afternoon nap than usual. As a result, dinner done and the dishes cleared away, I settled down in the living-room rocker to discover that the heap of printed matter on the table next to me contained nothing I hadn't read except some seed catalogs. These are not my idea of fun—and besides, anything remotely of interest in them (and much of no interest whatsoever) had already been read to me by the Woman Warrior—so I went upstairs to the library, where I settled on Compton Mackenzie's *Sinister Street*.

I had a fine time with it. Despite its lurid title, *Sinister Street* is a classic *bildungsroman* of upper-class English life on the cusp between Victoria and Edward. It is, of course, ethnocentric, snobbish, sexist, and sentimental, but also as touching in its stammering way as awkward youths themselves. I would not have used this last phrase when I first read the book some fifteen or twenty years ago, but now that I've settled into an extraordinarily graceful middle age, I can afford to take youth less seriously than I did when I still had some.

It was the pleasures of *Sinister Street* that got me thinking about the pleasures of a library. The Estragon Collection (as it is known virtually nowhere) is the usual higgledy-piggledy assemblage of a print junkie who has had the good fortune either to live or to work near good used-books stores for more than twenty years. As such, it is befittingly arrayed on ill-painted shelves purchased from one of the ubiquitous Greek outlets on 14th Street and is housed, since its merger with the Warrior Archives, in our attic.

But the attic is finished and heated, and holds a couple of comfortable chairs as well. It's a warm place not only because heat rises but because the books themselves are reliable old friends. In a way, they're more reliable than friends; if a fondly remembered favorite disappoints me, it's because I've changed and not because some quarto has taken to wearing gold medallions on its hairy chest. Similarly, books are at liberty to improve with (my) age, and I can always browse among them to see how they're coming along.

In the face of such paradoxical permanence, my obsession with something as evanescent as dinner feels a little ludicrous. Upstairs, there is the immutability of the ages; downstairs, a few leftover bones and some greasy plates. One can never revisit a dinner spoiled by a foul mood and do it proper justice.

All in all, skipping over the problem of storage, this is not such a bad thing. I suppose there are cooks who cringe when the knife slices through a capon's nut-brown skin and destroys the tableau, but I am not among them. I've never believed as much in the joy of cooking as the joys of eating and of sharing food with the people I love.

At dinner, the magic is in the air as well as on the plate, but aside from certain public events (and perhaps those moments when amusement or indignation practically forces one to read something aloud), reading is exclusionary. I can recall, when my sons were younger, their absolute *fury* whenever I got the giggles over a book; once, indeed, the Potato King spirited away my open Wodehouse novel and blacked out several pages with purple crayon. I was angry, of course, and he either got spanked or confined to his room, but I understood how he felt.

Since dinner is at some level *about* sharing, one would expect the sense of sadness that occurs when the family leaves the table for its various pursuits, or when the last dinner guest has been packed off to the subway, to be overwhelming, but it is balanced by the pleasant well-being provided by a full tum. If anything, the pain of finishing a book—though it will still be on the shelves the next morning—is more intense. It is not only after coitus that living creatures are sad, and no matter how tired I am when I finish a book, I always try to get at least a start on another before I go to bed. Which we do, appropriately enough, midway between the kitchen and the library.

CURRIED CHICKEN SALAD

This room-temperature dish is particularly useful for dinners during our sporadic bursts of false spring, for though it is quite substantial, it at least hints toward the days when people will claim they're too hot to eat.

1. Split 2 chicken breasts, sprinkle the pieces with lemon juice and a couple cloves of chopped garlic, broil them until just barely done (15 to 20 minutes at the outside), and set aside.

2. While they're cooking, prepare ½ cup rice in the usual manner, ditto about 2 cups peas. Drain the peas and set them to cool, mixing the rice in with them when it's done. Add to this about ½ cup raisins (plumped, if necessary, for a minute or so in warm water).

3. Remove the skin from the broiled chicken pieces (eat it on the spot: cook's privilege), and tear the meat from the bones in bite-sized chunks. Stir into the rice/pea/raisin mixture along with small chopped onion.

4. Prepare 1 cup or so of mayonnaise (or, in a pinch, use bot-

tled), and gradually blend into it anywhere from 1 to 4 tablespoons curry powder (or mix-your-own curry). The vaguer than usual quantity here is because prepared curry powders differ widely in flavor and fire, and you want the mayonnaise to have a little bite. Fresh grated ginger may help if it seems to you to lack oomph.

5. Mix the mayonnaise in with the other ingredients; serve with a bread.

6. Eat it all. Refrigerated curries cannot go home again.

Serves 4.

Fellow Travelers

I was doing all right answering the questions on the passport application until I got to "height." Then I started to giggle. But I recovered and soberly filled in the required information: two feet, one inch. The Youngest Member was going to England with us.

We were going because a magazine wondrously decided that I would be a swell person to look at tennis players for them. The Youngest Member's reason for traveling was, as I wrote on her behalf, "to accompany parents." Since one of these parents is her primary food source, her decision seemed plausible enough, and I figured she'd breeze through customs.

In fact, I wasn't worried about her at all—except for what I feared jet lag might do to her already overflexible schedule. It was her brothers I worried about. For two weeks, they'd be on their own.

More or less. They had copious written instructions—all the way down to "Eat your vegetables" and "Don't forget to feed *and water* the cats"—and the neighbors agreed to keep half an eye on things. My sister was going to check in from time to time, too. (They will be all right. They're practically grown-ups. They shave. I am whistling past the graveyard.)

All these preliminary doodads had been attended to, and my uneasiness about leaving them alone had settled into a manageable simmer, when we got a letter from the Potato King's high school. It invited us to "share the joy" of watching him receive an award at something called Senior Recognition Night.

Naturally, this plunged me into despair. One couldn't very well add yet another instruction ("Tuesday night: Share joy") to the already imposing list, and I began to imagine an incredibly festive occasion, clusters of families and flashbulbs and popping champagne corks, with the Potato King alone in a corner, bravely wiping away a tear with the edge of his elaborately inscribed scroll.

This was, I knew, an exaggeration. I have attended enough events of this sort to know that the kids all hang out together anyway. But I still fretted. Should we postpone the trip? Indeed, could we? (The tennis players would move on, and it was they who were indirectly providing me the wherewithal to pay my backbreaking share of the Potato King's college tuition.)

Besides, when you get down to it, I wanted to visit England. It was there, seven years ago, that I stopped being unemployed and started being a writer, so it has a special attraction for me. Not anything so dramatic as Castaneda's "power spot"—I can always do a little acid and find one of those—but mystical nonetheless.

It's precisely because I wanted to go that I felt bad. If the tennis players had been in Columbus, Ohio, I could have felt virtuous. You know, there-is-my-firstborn-receiving-an-award-and-I'm-out-here-suffering. But visions of England, where there's wonderful Indian food and my friends all talk like Dr. Pressclips, produced nothing but guilt.

Out of the depths I bethought me of O'Brian. He is the Potato King's godfather and takes his work with a proper sense of responsibility. Long ago, at St. Brigid's Church on Avenue B, O'Brian had doubtfully held a squalling infant in his arms (though it seems improbable to look at him now, the Potato King was nattily turned out in a long, white christening dress) and allowed as how this baby was forever renouncing the devil's pomps and snares.

In the intervening years, O'Brian has tended the Potato King's spiritual well-being mostly by listening to his complaints about me and agreeing with them. He has also, since his own tastes run toward potatoes, been responsible for my preparing some dinners that the Potato King has found more tolerable than usual. Interrupted at his work of hounding debtors, O'Brian agreed that sharing joy certainly fell under the godfathering rubric, and signed on for Senior Recognition Night.

He further offered to take the Potato King to dinner that evening, leaving me to travel guilt-free, secure in the knowledge that a few hours after I've pigged down some of the Standard's wonderful *keema nan*, those two will be answering the waiter's, "mashed, boiled, or french fried?" with an enthusiastic "Yes."

Not that our trip was devoid of troublesome incident. In fact, the Youngest Member developed a cold while we were in England, and with it, her very own baby boogers. Since she had not yet mastered the art of finding her nose, they remained, ripe for the picking, until one of us removed them.

To some this activity may seem less than attractive. One night, when I must have been about two or three years old and my mother was putting me to bed, she saw an odd pattern on the side of my dresser. She'd noticed something before, but it seemed to have grown. Puzzled, she asked if I knew what it was. "A Christmas tree," I said proudly. And sure enough, when she looked closely, it did bear a passing resemblance to the child's classic hard-edged pine tree. Had she been content to let well enough alone, my artistic ability might have flourished, but she was curious—not to say uneasy—about my chosen medium. Allowing that it was a handsome tree indeed, she asked what I'd been using to make it. "Boogers," I said, and by way of illustration dug my finger into my nose and judiciously added another ornament to the design. "Yecch," she said, and by morning she had Bon Ami'd my tree into oblivion.

Our reaction, however, was quite the opposite of "yecch." Picking someone else's nose turns out to be a curiously satisfying task. It is humane—the baby literally breathes easier—relatively clean, and when the nasal passage is cleared, there's a sense of a job well done. And so, for reasons hygienic and aesthetic we did our best. Q-tips, a nose syringe, the odd finger . . . nothing was too good for her. You'd have thought she'd be grateful.

But no. Though babies in general, and the Youngest Member in specific, adore being fussed over (did you know about the experiment in which nurses, when they removed infants' wet diapers, sometimes put the same ones back on instead of changing them for new? The babies, satisfied by the attention, were utterly indifferent to wet and dry), the Youngest Member found all this to be too much of a muchness. By the time her cold hit Day Three, the mere sight of the bright-blue bulb on the nose syringe was enough to start her kicking and screaming. Which soon turned out to be the way we felt about dinner.

Under the best of circumstances, dining in public with the Youngest Member was tricky. Five months old, she could no longer be counted on to slumber in one's lap for the length of a meal but was too young to understand conventional notions of civility. When she was hungry/tired/bored, she let us know it. Loudly. Though there were a couple of neighborhood restaurants prepared to accommodate us during their off-hours, we pretty much abandoned eating out for the duration. Though I too like being fussed over, the knowledge that Estragon's traveling circus can ruin dinner for quite a large group of inoffensive strangers kept us generally at home.

Which was easy enough in Brooklyn (home is where the kitchen is), but considerably more difficult in a hotel room in a strange city. With a baby who can't go out anyway because she has a cold and it's raining again today. In such circumstances, take-away fish and chips rapidly begin to exhibit declining marginal utility. And so we called room service.

In this hotel (the fancy-dancy one chosen by the organizers of the tennis tournament), when you tell room service you want dinner, they say, "Certainly," and hang up. The next thing you know, there is a man in a dinner jacket entering your room. He has menus with him, and a thick, leather-bound wine list. You discuss, he suggests ... the smoked trout perhaps, the turtle soup, the roast lamb with its attendant array of potatoes, the cheese, the sweet ... the table appears, nine pieces of silver at each place ... and, one course at a time, the meal. We dined, looking out across the Channel, to the distant music of the Cheshire Regimentals tootling away in the Victorian band shell, and for a while, it was possible to forget we were eating *haute* hotel.

But along about the third day of this incredible luxury, a sort of high-class cabin fever set in. On the way to work in the mornings I regularly passed a greengrocer's, his windows stacked with shining pea pods, jewel-like tiny raspberries, crisp spatulate broad beans, deliquescent strawberries. Each, in its perfection, seemed to mock me; I was never going to cook them, and they might as well have been produced by Claes Oldenburg. At night, back in the hotel, as the waiter uncovered yet another platter, I began to understand why the Youngest Member didn't think it was all that much fun to have someone pick her nose for her.

SAUTÉED NEW POTATOES

We had, of course, laid in a generous supply of potatoes against our absence, and this simple and quite delicious dish often accompanied the chicken breasts, ham steak, pork chops, hamburgers, etc. in the freezer.

1. For 4 people, carefully scrub 1½ lbs. new potatoes, slice them thin—about 6 slices to the inch—and put them in a pot of cold water. Add salt, and bring the water to the boil for no more than 2 to 3 minutes.

2. In a heavy skillet, sauté 1 medium-sized chopped onion over *low* heat in 2 tablespoons of vegetable oil and a half-stick butter until the onion softens. 3. Drain the potatoes thoroughly and add them to the skillet. Add salt generously, and pepper to taste. Keeping the heat low, continue cooking, turning them frequently, until they get wonderfully crispy. This will take some time, perhaps 15 minutes, but it's worth the wait. At the last minute, sprinkle with dill and serve.

CHICKEN AND AVOCADO SALAD

One thing absent from my fantasies of home was the heat. We left Eastbourne bundled in sweaters against the chill and arrived in New York to find it 92 degrees. So our first home-cooked meal was this salad, which hardly counts as cooking at all. But even with the passing D trains in place of the regimental band, it was delicious.

1. Cover a whole chicken with water and bring it to a boil. Throw out the water, including its yucky gray scum, rinse the chicken in cool water, and begin the process again. This time, use a little less water, and add to it 1 glass white wine, 1 peeled onion, 2 small carrots, 1 large rib celery, salt, and 6 peppercorns. Allow to simmer slowly for 25 to 30 minutes, then remove the chicken and let it cool. Save the stock for another night's soup.

2. Tear a small head of romaine into manageable pieces and put them in a salad bowl along with 1 ripe avocado of large but not monstrous size. Add torn-off bits of about half the poached chicken (the rest is for that cold cream of chicken curry soup), and crumble 4 ounces blue cheese over the whole thing. Dress with the juice of 1 lemon mixed with 6 ounces olive oil and 1 egg yolk. Blend thoroughly and top, at the last minute, with fresh, hot, garlicky croutons. Serves 4.

Cannery Row

*I*probably wasn't paying as much attention to the Youngest Member as I should have been—I was in fact, ignoring her completely as I tried to figure out just how the folks at Citibank's "escrow analysis" unit were screwing us—but after a while, I noticed the absence of her phonemically catholic babble. I also noticed, from the kitchen, a noise rather like wind chimes. There are no wind chimes in our kitchen.

I scooted out there and found the Youngest Member happily building a tower of sherbet glasses. As she slammed the fifth one down on the four she'd already assembled into a Pisan vertical, I froze. It balanced there; nothing had shattered as yet, and she wasn't bleeding. "*Good* baby," I cooed, stealthily advancing toward her, "*clever* baby." She interrupted her construction work to give herself a round of applause. I joined in, clapping and cooing, until I got close enough to scoop her up. "*Good* baby. Let's go back into the living room and see how many blocks you can build with."

We played together with her blocks for a bit, and when she'd gotten thoroughly caught up in construction work, I snuck back and looked for a safe place to stash the glasses. Finding none, I heaped them in the center of the kitchen table and returned to the living room, where I solaced myself with the thought that by the time the bank finally gears itself up to snatch our house away, she'll probably have wrecked it.

That night, after she'd gone to bed, we rearranged the kitchen. Again. Into the hitherto impregnable bottom of the hutch went the muffin tins and baking pans; glass and pottery took their place in the upper reaches of the pantry. At some point during this process (which has gone on piecemeal with each advance in her coordination), I began thinking about my own childhood kitchen play and realized that our household is woefully short of cans.

Cans were fun. You could roll them, stack them, hammer with them, tear their labels off (heh, heh), even use them as furniture. When you consider how versatile cans are, it's obvious we don't have enough of them. My parents used to buy canned coffee (Martinson's Red); we use bagged Bustelo. I always got to play with juice cans; we drink either frozen or fresh-squoze. Finally, my parents' pantry was lined with rows of canned fruits and vegetables; we keep a couple of cans of Italian tomatoes on hand, but that's about it. With tuna fish and corned beef hash about the only ties to my youth, we are clearly depriving the Youngest Member of an important toddler pleasure. (On the other hand, we aren't making her eat canned fruit cocktail either, so she probably won't be able to win a neglect case in Family Court.)

This paucity of cans isn't a result of the much-touted packaging revolution; a trip through the supermarket doesn't reveal Cyrovac envelopes of mandarin orange slices or kadota figs. To the extent that technology rather than taste is involved, it has provided alternatives to what's inside the cans, not to the cans themselves. Hybridization has led to longer growing seasons for fresh produce, and though frozen vegetables are usually (but not always) a poor alternative to fresh, they are several orders of magnitude closer to nature than are the gray squishy ones that come in cans. In a pinch, I sometimes use frozen peas, but I don't think I've *ever* bought canned.

But even though I can't imagine willingly eating the stuff, I sometimes think we should buy some. Not only were the labels on canned goods among my earliest sources of culinary information, but they probably also taught me something about abstraction. Baby bottles of strained juice carry pictures of whole fruits which the Youngest Member studies intently, and I suspect her mind is busy forming linkages as she does so. That she doesn't get to go through similar processes with dozens of different canned goods is too bad, in a way, but she'll survive. Besides, if I allow myself to get all choked up over it, I'll wind up complaining that there's no longer enough horse shit in the streets.

ROAST LAMB WITH FLAGEOLETS AND ESCAROLE

Listen, it's not easy finding a recipe that uses canned goods. Eggs Sardou was a possibility, but that's not so much a recipe as a concept (poached egg on artichoke bottoms on bed of creamed spinach, whole thing covered with hollandaise). This one, though you could just as well substitute slightly underdone dried baby limas for the flageolets, was the best I could do. It's delicious.

1. Preheat oven to 325 degrees, stud a 5 to 6 lb. leg of lamb with at least 2 large cloves of garlic, slivered. Salt and pepper the meat, dust it with curry powder, and put it in the oven in a roasting pan to which you've added about ½ cup mild beef stock. Cook, basting occasionally with the pan liquids, until a meat thermometer registers 150 degrees (allow about 25 minutes a pound).

2. When the lamb is almost done, remove the floppy tops and stem from 1 medium head of escarole and chop the rest into bite-sized chunks. Mix these with ¼ cup of olive oil, wine vinegar, dry mustard, 2 more larger cloves of garlic—and another ½ cup of beef stock. Rinse 2 15-oz. cans of imported flageolets and add them to the escarole.

3. When the lamb is done, surround it in the pan with the

escarole/flageolet combine, stir the veg around in the lamb juices, then turn the oven off and let them sit together, door closed, for 15 to 20 minutes. (Serves 4 comfortably, leaving one or two leftover meals. We had lamb and eggplant curry and a sort of shepherd's pie.)

Please Disturb

I've been getting ready to go out of town on a story, and part of the drill involved making a major supermarket trip that would keep the household in staples during my week-long jaunt. Putting together the shopping list meant laying out a week's menus, and I was a little surprised to hear the Woman Warrior announce there would be "one night of potato pancakes, one of pizza, and one of Chinese food. That's one of our rituals whenever you're gone." I didn't like the idea of any rituals going on behind my back; household rites should include me, or they shouldn't happen at all.

Yet I suppose my occasional trips are just regular enough that a stay-at-home drill is in order. Lord knows I go through my own bits of business. At home, we last watched the *Today* show in order to learn the magnitude of Reagan's electoral sweep; alone in my hotel room, it is a comforting morning human-noise. Indeed, every recurring shift in our domestic lineup has led to some formal celebration or mourning of the new situation. The Potato King has been away at college only since September, but each homecoming and departure is marked by a dinner built around his favorites; the same thing will no doubt happen when the Mad Baker leaves for college. And of course when they're both in town and go off to visit their mother for a weekend, the Woman Warrior and I feast on all the foods we've been unable to sneak past their chorused "yecch."

Still, I don't like going away. A few weeks ago, I was talking about matters domestic with a *Voice* writer who said he couldn't understand how committed couples *ever* allowed themselves to sleep apart. He simply doesn't take on out-of-town assignments unless his wife is free to travel with him. I find something admirable in this stance—passionate monogamy is not a wildly popular position in *Voice* circles—but I don't think I could live that way, and it doesn't make me particularly happy to examine why.

When I strip away the various rationales (unlike us, they have money in the bank and are at the moment childless) I'm stuck with the realization that I probably value work—a job, "the story"—more than is good for me. Would any story have been worth missing the Youngest Member's virtually overnight transition from infant to toddler? It did happen very fast. After what seemed like weeks of standing up and moving with one hand or the other always firmly attached to a piece of furniture, she suddenly made the leap of faith and let go. Three days later, she was walking everywhere and had put crawling behind her forever. "Scoop" Estragon was there to cover the event, and I'm glad.

But ol' Scoop can't be home all the time. I have to go out and get cigarettes, for instance. Also, since baby does indeed need new shoes, I have to earn them. But that's in the nature of a rationale as well; I'm sure if I just set my mind to it I could stay home and write the Adequate American Novel. The thing is, for reasons of ego that I can only classify as masculine, I'm afraid. If I wasn't being *something*, I wouldn't be anything.

To some degree, the Woman Warrior believes that as well—one reason among many why she's increasingly eager to be back on the streets with her reporter's notebook—but she finds a solace in parent's work that I don't. She *knows* it's a job; I think of it as something one does on the side.

And as I did my own ritual packing—paperbacks for any solitary dinners, fat novels for late at night—I began to feel that somewhere along the line, I'd been cheated. Later, alone in a hotel room, I'd realize I was cheating myself.

～～～～～

STEAK DIANE

My own homecoming dinner will be special as well—and because I'm scheduled to arrive late at night, its elegance will be *à deux*. This version of steak Diane is less flashy than many (literally, for the cognac isn't flamed), but certainly celebratory.

1. Pound 2 one-inch club steaks (about ¾ lb. each) until they're about half their original thickness. Pepper each side generously, and sauté them over high heat in about 2 tablespoons butter and a little oil (for rare, about 3 minutes on one side, half that time on the second).

2. Remove the steaks, and quickly add to the pan, off the heat, 3 or 4 chopped shallots. Stir them around for 10 or 15 seconds, then pour in 3 to 4 oz. dry sherry and a short shot of cognac. Return the pan to the heat, and scrape all the brown bits off the bottom into the sherry/cognac mixture. After 2 or 3 minutes, toss in a half-handful of chopped parsley and a little—no more than a teaspoon—Dijon mustard. Stir just long enough to mix, then add another tablespoon of butter, and swirl it around. Pour the sauce over the meat as soon as the butter has melted, and before it has returned to a boil.

3. Asparagus with a little lemon juice and olive oil is perfect with this dish, but any fresh green vegetable would make someone especially glad to be home again.

Labored Relations

I've been working on a book for the past few months, an activity (if that's the proper term for endless staring at an electric typewriter) that has kept me off the streets and in despair. During the first week or so of this enterprise, the Woman Warrior and I kept tripping over each other, for none of our previous domestic routines had included me brooding about the battlements. I used to be home fairly often, but usually for periods scheduled to coincide with the Woman Warrior's street-reporting, and if I wasn't exactly the captain of my soul, I was at any rate the only adult in the house and could pretty much do what I wanted. And when I was at the office, ditto for her.

No longer. There remain days when she vanishes with the commuters and returns home just in time for dinner—and every now and then, I break training and go out for a fancy lunch with a publisher—but often we're both at home, both with paying work to be done, and both with a toddler to nurture. Gradually, a schedule has evolved that has me working from about five in the morning until whatever time the Youngest Member begins chirping (usually seven or seven-thirty). The next couple of hours are shared time—coffee, newspapers, chatter, breakfast—and by ten, the Woman Warrior is at work as a writer and

I as a father. At one we swap (not exactly an even-up trade, for she gets to become a mother, a job with different perks). All in all, I even like staring at a typewriter better than being a househusband. Though the Youngest Member is a sparkling conversationalist, her recognizable vocabulary consists of about twenty words, and much of her ceaseless stream of information and instruction is frustratingly unintelligible. Frustrating to me, at any rate; she continues to gabble undaunted, sure that I'll eventually shape up and figure out what she's saying. But until I do, I'll continue to feel vaguely dislocated. And dependent.

That's the rub. It's impossible to read seriously when one is watching a toddler (it's possible, actually, but the whole idea is to be *with* her), so even in the relatively short on-duty time of three or four hours, I find myself missing interchange with adults. The radio helps, but to get the deejay's patter, you have to put up with the deejay's choice of music and a little bit of Van Halen goes a very very long way. So I end up playing records, which is fun (and until you've heard the Youngest Member sing along with Johnny Lydon on PIL's latest, you ain't heard nothin'), but it isn't precisely conversation.

The mail comes around ten-thirty, but its contents are often disappointing. Still, those moments between the clicking of the door slot and my discovery that I've mysteriously gotten on the Cousteau Society's mailing list are the morning's peak. Unless the Woman Warrior comes downstairs for coffee.

But welcome as those respites are, they serve to underscore my dependence; whichever of us is scheduled to work is free to come play with the other, but the worker's office is off-limits to the on-duty parent. I chafe.

I also fantasize lunch. Not so much the food—often just last night's leftovers heated up, or an egg salad sandwich—but the event. A real lunch has its functional child-rearing aspect—it makes the Youngest Member's role during the exchange of responsibilities a little less like that of the baton during a relay race—and it serves the adults as well. It is a cushion that eases our transitions from one role to another, a chance for Daddy to do his own version of unintelligible babble, and for Mommy to get caught up on the dramas of the morning.

And then I go upstairs to do what I've been dreaming about for hours. Downstairs, or sometimes faintly through the window, I hear the conversation going on without me and wish that it were still morning. Men, what do they want?

~~~~~~

PARSLEY BREAD

This was a more or less typical lunch, involving leftovers from two different dinners. It could, however, be made from scratch, and in any case, keeping a couple of composed butters in the refrigerator is not a bad idea.

This one, which had first done duty on a grilled chicken, began with 1 stick of salt butter creamed with 3 large cloves of mashed peeled garlic, a generous half-handful of chopped parsley, and 3 or 4 chopped basil leaves. With the addition of a couple of tablespoons of grated Parmesan, some of the leftovers went into grilled whole tomatoes, the rest was thickly smeared on a half-loaf of thickly crusted Italian bread (cut lengthwise) and heated in a 400-degree oven for about 10 minutes.

This would have been a fine accompaniment to any relatively mild main dish, but made a perfectly swell lunch all on its own. With a little chilled Soave. In the back yard. Yum.

Counting the Seconds

*O*ne o'clock. Time for the Woman Warrior to relinquish
her typewriter and take over dandling duties. The
Youngest Member and I stand at the foot of the stairs and call
up to her (the Youngest Member is considerably less tall than I,
but she's very sincere). Eventually, the Woman Warrior appears,
and there's an outbreak of hugging, kissing, and hand clapping.
Also information exchange: "What did *you* do this morning,
baby? Did you have a *good* morning with Daddy?" The Youngest Member, having done her famous monkey-up-a-flagpole
imitation on her mother, nods vigorously and smashes her forehead into the maternal nose. Such little contretemps are all in a
day's parenting, however, and as soon as the anguished howls
subside, I am called upon to give a more complete rendering of
the morning's activities. I get to do this because I can talk whole
sentences at a time.

But the Youngest Member has become a champion nodder, so
the rehearsal is carried out in interrogatories from me and head-
bobs from her (Contrary to baby-book theory, she has "yes"
down pat, but "no" has yet to emerge; disagreement is conveyed
by the absence of agreement. Thus, "Did we play in the yard?"
gets a nod, but "Did we snort coke and paint the cat red?" earns
only a blank stare. I test her like that just to make sure she's not

faking.) Gradually we work our way through outdoor play, two diaper changes, the arrival of a sanitation truck, and wind up with lunch: "Did you have *potato* pie? . . . *That's* right, and did you have *melon*? . . . *That's* right, and did you have peanut-butter-and-banana *too*? . . . That's *right*. What a *good* lunch you had."

It really was a good lunch, and since the Youngest Member is an eccentric eater, I expect congratulations for my persistence in getting her satisfactorily stuffed. I don't get them.

"She ate the potato pie?"

"Yes."

"*All* the potato pie?"

"Yup."

"Shit. What are *we* going to have for lunch?"

Blank stare.

Later, grimly chewing my peanut-butter-and-jelly sandwich, I remember how we couldn't wait until she stopped eating baby food, and talked about what fun it would be to introduce her to grown-up food. It *is* fun, it turns out, but there are these drawbacks. Mostly because we don't know what she'll like (or if she'll even deign to taste today what she only yesterday swore up and down she loved), we certainly can't count on any leftovers from her. This is a drag, for one of food's great pleasures is anticipation.

It operates at the top of the aesthetic ladder—when the Woman Warrior and I are going out for some celebratory occasion, we debate the restaurant *weeks* in advance—and on quotidian levels as well. When I was a kid, dinner on the nights when I knew there was a hand-dipped quart of Breyer's vanilla fudge in the freezer was a qualitatively different kind of experience. Anticipation transformed the so-called main course into a particularly ornate foreplay that made the decision about second helpings deliciously difficult.

Finally, it works on day-after-everyday levels. When I wrap up a particularly fine leftover and stash it in the refrigerator, I'm already imagining the moment when I'll unwrap it. Sometimes, I confess, I've lusted so for that moment that I've not only wrapped the morsel up, but hidden it away in a corner so no one else will find it. Now, however, betrayed by love (and, of course, my exquisite sense of honor), I leave my treasures in plain sight, eating them only if they survive the Youngest Member's lunch unscathed. I miss the anticipation, but that loss is as nothing compared to what I feel when someone else gets them before I do.

~~~~~~~~

ITALIAN POTATO PIE

This recipe serves 4 very generously, and makes swell leftovers.

1. Boil 4 *large* potatoes and mash them with milk, butter, pepper, oregano, a little salt, and a little nutmeg; they should be smooth, but fluffy rather than sticky. Butter a large glass or ceramic pie plate, cover the bottom and sides with breadcrumbs, and line the plate with a little less than half the potatoes.

2. Fill the potato pocket with ½ lb. coarsely julienned prosciutto and ¼ to ½ lb. julienned cheese. The version that vanished in the Youngest Member's lunch was half mozzarella, half provolone, but Bel Paese or fontina are elegantly acceptable alternatives. Arrange, according to your own painterly preference, 2 or 3 hard-boiled egg halves on top of the prosciutto-cheese heap.

3. Close the pie with the rest of the potatoes (praying that you've made enough to begin with), sprinkle the top with breadcrumbs, dot it generously with butter, and bake it in a hot (400-degree) oven for 20 to 25 minutes. A simple green salad is plenty with this.

Leaving a Note
That I Hoped Would
Say More

O nce upon a time and a very good time it was there was
a paperboy coming down the road and this paperboy
that was coming down along the road met almost nobody because it was early in the morning but he made a nice thump anyway when he dropped his heavy Sunday newspapers on the
porch and woke me up.

I didn't mind; unless I'm hung over, there can never be too
much Sunday morning. And so, sneaking out of bed so as not to
disturb the Woman Warrior, I descended for the day's first coffee. After extricating my legs from the importunate cats—when
it comes to his morning Tender Vittles, Mick doesn't take
"soon" for an answer—I sat, alone, and read. All in all, a typical
Sunday morning (of the pre–Youngest-Member era; she tends to
be up with the birdies and the paperboys), and as I recall it, my
solitude lasted for about two cups of coffee and three newspaper
sections (sports and books from the *Times*, comics from the
News).

First there was a distant radio, then a flushing toilet and a
splashing shower, and finally the wall-shaking vibrations of a
teen-ager coming downstairs as quietly as he could. Soon after
the process repeated itself with the Potato King's entrance, the

papers were well into their dance from chair to chair and I was in the kitchen making up a tray. Nothing elegant, just juice and coffee, but a tray nonetheless. Then, gathering up the sections of the *Times* that offended the sensibilities of youth (i.e., most of it) and whatever they'd finished of the *News*, I went to wake the Woman Warrior.

We sipped coffee, cuddled, traded tidbits of amusement and outrage from the journalistic world, and—after a decent interval—began to consider breakfast. Sunday breakfasts are worth thinking about. They're obviously different from the variously timed scavenges that serve breakfasts' purposes during the week, but they're unlike Saturday's as well. Sure, we're usually all home on Saturday, but the day comes complete with its scheduled list of errands: things to be lugged to and from the dry cleaners, complicated purchases to be negotiated at the hardware store, a floor or two to be washed. . . .

Sundays are better. Unless one counts the Giants' weekly humiliation on TV, the days stretch out empty, virtually begging to be filled with food. Especially with a late, lazy breakfast—the participants, still in bathrobes, sitting over fresh juice and savoring the smell of sausage.

But that particular Sunday was different. When we came down to start cooking, things seemed a little bustlier than usual, and by the time the Woman Warrior had put together her pancake batter, both kids were already dressed. One was off to the library to work on a term paper, the other to picnic with friends somewhere on Staten Island. But couldn't they stay for breakfast? Nope. Things to do, people to see. "I had a bagel." "I had some cereal." G'bye.

One knows all along, of course, that one's children will eventually leave home, but there are times when that knowledge delivers a sucker punch. Sitting at the breakfast table, watching the half-full bowl of raw batter dry around the edges, I found myself thinking not of elegant brunches to come but of empty places at the table. I didn't get all unstrung by the fantasy (in fact, I suspected even at the time that it was a bit of masochistic self-indulgence), but soon enough, life began to imitate art, for the Potato King began making his college plans.

A couple of years ago, the house was full of those visions and dreams. Armed with glossy pamphlets and his SAT scores, the Potato King imagined going off to some college that combined the best features of *Animal House*, *The Halls of Ivy*, and the late show at the Ritz. My somewhat grimmer fantasies, prompted by a terrifying peek at the financial information in his catalogs, involved debtor's prison and the poorhouse.

But I was comforted with smells, for as the Potato King retreated into a private world of acronyms, percentiles, and recondite discussions of average faculty salaries, the junior Tasteless One so busied himself in the kitchen that he came to be called the Mad Baker. (And how did the Potato King get to be the Potato King? Easy. When I was ten or eleven years old and first learning my way around the stove, I regularly feasted on a Saturday midmorning breakfast of hot buttered noodles. For this perfectly amiable eccentricity, I earned the family nickname of the Noodle King. Hence . . .)

Point is, the kid was good. None of this choke-it-down-so-you-don't-discourage-the-child stuff—"My, these certainly are *interesting* brownies. And weren't you *clever* to think of using bacon grease when you ran out of butter?"—just flat-out enjoyment at the parade of apple pies that emerged from his efforts to perfect his crust.

His breads were even better than his pies. Mostly because of their versatility. Sure, banana bread is a perfectly acceptable dessert, but you can also eat it for breakfast without the guilty twinge that accompanies an early-morning slice of banana cream pie. (Wait a second. You're talking to the former Noodle King, here. Pie is perfectly capable of being eaten for breakfast—it wishes merely to please and is indifferent to the hour—and the problem isn't pie's lack of flexibility but my stuffiness.) I suppose I'll have to practice. (Heh heh.)

But, like apple pies and banana bread, some things are too

good to last, and I anticipated that the cornucopia of baked goods would abruptly empty as soon as the Potato King had settled down with a nice comfortable college. There has always been a certain seesaw logic to the kids' Cain-and-Abel routines, and I figured that when it came time for the Mad Baker's bout of college anxiety, I'd be back to store-bought English muffins. The time came sooner than I expected. But life with the Tasteless Ones is full of surprises (I can even recall there sometimes being a dry towel left in the bathroom after their morning ablutions), and the baking habit seems to have stuck. I got worried, though, when the Mad Baker interrupted my consideration of one of his pies to remark that *his* high school was having a college night and we should go to it so he could make plans for his future.

I agreed (I mean, what else could I do? "No, no, my son. Stay home and make me fat"?), and even managed to work up a perfunctory question about what he thought he might want to study.

"Restaurant management," he answered.

Well, lordy. Or as Chuck Berry put it, " '*C'est la vie,*' said the old folks. 'It goes to show you never can tell.' "

Which indeed you can't. The Mad Baker, pie output undiminished, wound up choosing a college that would rather curl up in its tiny experimental bed and *die* before teaching anything remotely practical. But even after all the baking had come to a stop, I really wouldn't have had any right to complain; when I started college, I wanted to be a lawyer, which is something I am emphatically not. Indeed, about the only thing that hasn't changed over the years is my fondness for food.

I recall an enlightening evening I spent several years ago— back when the boys were still living with their mother and visiting me only during school vacations—with a group of adults who picked vigorously at the remains of a capon and discussed the stratagems they'd once used to get around parental suggestions that they eat disgusting things like spinach or Brussels sprouts. The way they told it, their adolescence had been a never-ending struggle to slip their despised portion of calf's liver to a handy pet or sibling.

I was shocked. Not so much because the demolition job they'd done on my capon had belied any history of persnicketiness (though it had), but because the notion that one might actually not *want* to eat seemed so utterly foreign. My own adolescent dinners had usually concluded with me volunteering to clean the table so I could use the serving spoons for efficient private piggery. These people had not only attempted to avoid eating, they had cheated and lied to get out of it.

But when the boys came down from New Hampshire to live with me and the Woman Warrior, shock gave way to resignation. Although the deviousness of children is everywhere impressive (largely because they're so *serious* about it), it is positively spectacular at table. The kids always took too much of what they liked—thereby short-changing the rest of us (by which I guess I mean *me*)—and too little of what they disdained. Quizzed about the former, they lied; prompted about the latter, they attacked. At one point, I swore an oath before God and my readers that the next time some leaden-palated little Estragon referred to the capers in his hamburger as "green boogers," he was going to eat TV dinners for a week.

This sounds like I'm whining, doesn't it? I don't care. I'm entitled to a little whine now and then. After all, it wasn't as though we didn't try to anticipate their whims, but even if we'd been able to afford it, a cuisine of steak, french fries, frozen peas, and Haagen-Dazs would have paled after the first month or so. Besides, navigating their prejudices made the voyage between Scylla and Charybdis seem like an afternoon row in Central Park: The Mad Baker hated all seafood except shellfish, the Potato King eschewed any fish but flounder and sole; the Potato King craved ever more potatoes, the Mad Baker was dieting; the Mad Baker observed dryly that his chili was bland, the Potato King whooped for ice water. And so on.

Meanwhile, we waffled between rage and guilt. If we loved them, we'd fix things they liked, right? Yeah, and if they weren't hopelessly spoiled little snots, they'd eat what was on their plates and be grateful. You see the problem. Which was, of course, compounded when only one of them felt aggrieved; not only was he being maltreated, he always knew we loved his brother more anyway.

So we did tricks. Chinese food, with one favorite dish for each of them, was a useful dodge; pizzas with radically different trimmings another. And sometimes we just plain sold out, lowering the culinary common denominator to the point where we stood in serious danger of dining on Pringle's Potato Things and Seven-Up.

But sometimes we got lucky. One Sunday, knowing that Italian sausages weren't a big teen-age favorite, we figured we might be able to sneak them by if we combined them with good old chicken. It worked. We were pleased with the dinner, and the kids actually went back for seconds (in one case, thirds). Best, the chef received the ultimate accolade—"Good munchies, Dad"—a moment so gratifying I forebore mentioning that the compliment might better have been delivered with an empty mouth.

I was feeling so pleased with myself, in fact, that it wasn't until I heated some leftovers for Tuesday lunch that I realized the little bleeders had picked out all the chicken and left me with nothing but sausage. But I ate the sausage happily enough, complaining more for theatrical effect than anything else. I was probably even then getting ready for them to go. I missed so much of their lives' minutiae when they were living with their mother that it somehow doesn't seem fair they're already in college—that soon, when they say "home," they'll be talking about their own apartments instead of about this house.

The process had been underway for a while, I guess, but I didn't grasp its irreversibility until an April week when the Potato King got a stack of letters from colleges: thick missives welcoming him, thin ones politely regretting. Now one of them is sending me bills. I should have warned them he didn't eat eggs.

I mean, how can he read Virgil *ab ovo* if his professors have to disguise a metaphor as french toast? Is there no limit to the quest for relevance? Of pandering to the young? You never saw Fabergé enameling pieces of stale bread, did you? He knew a good thing when he saw one.

The Potato King still doesn't. But, as I was reminded the last time he came home, he doesn't know a bad one when he doesn't see it. Which is to say that an egg by any other name may well be okay. Spaghetti Carbonara, if he doesn't actually catch me mixing the egg yolk into the cheese, seems to taste good, and mozzarella *en carozza* (if I go easy on the anchovies) is perfectly acceptable. But your basic fried egg? Not on your life.

Maybe he's afraid he'll get egg on his face. Such fear is an occupational hazard of teen-agery, and rather a nice metaphor too, in its day. I often have egg on my face. I start out, you see, with this centrally located mustache that seems to have a fatal attraction for egg salad. The resulting effect is attractive neither to me nor to spectators.

It can, however, be remedied by a napkin. Imaginary egg lingers. Back in the late bronze age, when I was applying to college, I gauged my chances carefully, applying only to places I figured would be glad to have me. I had learned quite enough about rejection from the young ladies at Ursuline Academy, thank you, and I didn't need to get snooted by some institution.

The Potato King was braver than I. He figured out where he wanted to go and just went ahead and presented himself. The colleges responded with splendid unpredictability, creating a pattern of acceptance and rejection that seemed either random or Byzantine. Still, though the distribution of pain might be random, an accidental punch in the face hurts just as much as a deliberate one. But the Potato King handled rejection with courage and—more difficult—acceptance with grace. I was, it turned out, proud of him.

It may be that he had learned that the gulf between those thin envelopes and the fat ones is never so great as it appears. He had lived in a house where rejection slips are an all too palpable part of reality; the manuscript—one's lifeblood—is packed up, gets a new cover letter, and goes off again to take its chances in the world. It's not that the rejection doesn't hurt—it does, and besides, the mortgage is always due—but that an encrustation of imaginary egg is an inevitable condition of a writer's mustache. Even acceptance is often no more than rejection deferred. Divorce follows marriage; reviews follow publication; last week's crocuses are already gone. And don't forget letters to the editor.

I suppose, given all that nickel philosophy, I should have been more graceful when he rejected the eggs I cooked. Maybe fifteen or sixteen years from now I'll do better by the Youngest Member. Oh, old artificer, I don't believe that, let me tell you.

MIXED FRUIT TART

There are few things as challenging, and unappetizing, as unused pancake batter. It comforts the spirit not at all. Yet of this one, the Woman Warrior created so successful a metaphoric lemonade that the recipe is worth repeating. It could serve 4 as a light supper, 8 as dessert. Three of us made a disgustingly piggy sort of tea from it, and it was good enough that when the picnicker arrived home for dinner, his brother greeted him with, "Boy, did you miss something *great* today...."

Batter (from Anna Thomas's *Vegetarian Epicure*):

¾ cup unbleached white flour
½ tablespoon white sugar
a pinch salt
½ tablespoon baking powder
2 eggs, separated
1 cup milk
2 tablespoons melted butter.

Mix the dry ingredients together thoroughly, then add—mixed together—the egg yolks, milk, and melted butter. Stir until moist, then fold in the egg whites, beat until quite fluffy, but not dry.

Preheat oven to 400 degrees, then melt another generous tablespoon of butter in a heavy, cast-iron, 10-inch frying pan and pour the batter in all at once. When the bottom of the batter sets (perhaps two minutes), put the pan into the oven. It should be thoroughly cooked in about 15 minutes, but the toothpick-test is advisable.

While the cake is cooking, briskly sauté a selection of sliced, seasonal fruits (in midsummer, three peaches, two apples, and two bananas would be all right) in butter and brown sugar until warmed through. When the cake is done, slide it onto a platter, pour the fruit onto it, and cover the whole thing with 1 cup fresh cream, whipped. To serve, slice in wedges like a pie.

~~~~~~~~

THE MAD BAKER'S BANANA BREAD
(which sometimes has walnuts in it)

> 1 stick lightly salted butter
> 1 cup sugar
> 2 cups sifted flour
> 2 lightly beaten eggs
> 3 festering bananas
> ½ teaspoon salt
> 1 teaspoon baking soda
> ⅓ cup warm water

Melt butter over low heat, add sugar. Mash bananas and eggs together, add to sugar and butter mixture. Sift dry ingredients together, add to wet mixture alternately with water. Put in 9 × 5 greased loaf pan and bake at 375 degrees for 1 hour to 1 hour and 15 minutes.

~~~~~~~~

TWICE-SNUCK SAUSAGE

1. Saute 1 lb. *hot* Italian sausage, cut in ½-inch pieces, in a heavy frying pan until brown and crisp.

2. Add 2 boneless chicken breasts, cut into similar-sized chunks (and a little olive oil if the sausage has not given off enough fat), and brown them as well.

3. Pour in about 2 cups of hearty tomato sauce (the recipe for "Tomato Sauce I" in Marcella Hazan's wonderful *Classic Italian Cookbook* is recommended); reduce heat, cover, and simmer for about 10 minutes.

4. Serve with rottelli (or some other interestingly shaped pasta) that has been laved in butter and a generous grating of Romano.

~~~~~~~~

FARMER'S PIE

Accompanied by a simple green salad, this concoction makes a nice low-budget dinner, suitable equally to days when the mail holds more rejection slips than checks and to April nights that are suddenly cooler than the afternoons. Because it is full of things he likes, I figured I could sneak it by the Potato King; a covert glance seemed to indicate that I was right, but when he finally put down his fork I noticed that he had miraculously extracted a small pile of egg-bits and left them on a corner of his plate.

1. In a heavy frying pan, cook ½ lb. bacon until quite crisp; set aside on paper towels. Pour out all but a couple of tablespoons of the bacon fat and let the pan cool.

2. While it cools, peel and halve 3 medium onions. Cut them in thick slices and add them, with 2 tablespoons butter, to the frying pan. Cook very slowly, stirring occasionally, until they become translucent.

3. As the onion cooks, scrub and thinly slice 6 medium new potatoes. Put them in salted water and bring to a boil. Let boil for 3 or 4 minutes, then drain.

4. Add the potatoes to the frying pan; continue cooking until they start to crisp. Crumble the bacon and stir it into the potatoes and onions, along with a modest handful of chopped parsley. If the mixture seems to be sticking, add more butter.

5. Beat 9 eggs together and pour them into the pan. When the eggs have set on the bottom, set them on top by running the pan under the broiler for a couple of minutes. Serve in large wedges.

Philosofood

A Dissertation upon Roast Ambivalence

O ne of my family's nicer traditions was that the celebrant always got to choose the birthday menu. At first, I stuck with hamburgers and french fries, but as I increased in age and grace, I gradually expanded my requests: rib roast, capon, lobster ... expensive, yes, but only once a year. My father's tastes ran a varied round of more elaborately composed dishes, spicy exotica, which he often ended up making himself. Only my mother was constant; for her, roast pork and birthday were synonymous. Which proves that even mothers are not always wrong.

Pork, thanks to the relative efficiency of pigs as food processors, is humble in price, but noble in taste. Unless paranoiacally overcooked, it is unfailingly juicy. (*Trichinae* parasites are rendered harmless at an internal temperature of 137 degrees; when the meat is still a delicate pink at the center, it is perfectly safe—and delicious.) And pork is almost infinitely garnishable: apples, onions, thyme, rosemary, black pepper, even sour cream and paprika for a Hungarian *paprikash* complement it happily. The meat itself, as Charles Lamb described it more than 150 years ago in his "Dissertation Upon Roast Pig," is "fat and lean ... so blended and running into each other, that both together make one ambrosian result ..."

By imagining the primordial pig roast as accidental—the result of an unfortunate fire—Lamb sklithered past the awkward transition from live pig to roasted pork. As city dwellers, we have much the same luxury, for we are insulated from the barnyard origins of our dinners, and the neat ranks of plastic packages in our supermarket meat cases conspire to keep us that way. So despite my abiding fondness for pork, it was with some discomfort that I recently found myself in Shelter Island, grimly clutching the forelegs of a screaming, struggling pig while my neighbor's knife carefully searched her throat for the proper point of entry.

He found it, and as the first gush of blood crimsoned his hand and half his forearm, I found myself thinking—weirdly, perhaps in an attempt to reestablish that familiar urban distance—"So *that's* what 'bled like a stuck pig' means." With that, the doomed pig began to thrash violently, and reflection abruptly ended. With each frantic contraction, another gout of blood spurted from the jagged hole in her throat. "Hold the bastard tight," yelled the man who was grappling with her rear legs, "but let him kick. The more he kicks, the quicker the sombitch'll die."

At that moment, the pig—which a day earlier had both a name and a gender, and whose diet had indeed been an object of lively concern to her executioners—had become "bastard," "sombitch," "him" . . . and the unwilling participant in a ritual older than history.

At least she had for the other men. It was, after all, *their* ritual. They are longtime islanders, sons and grandsons of farmers who lived off these lands and seas. Though there's less farming on the island now—and more construction labor building second homes for Manhattanites—the cycle of birth, husbandry, and slaughter remains as familiar to them as the change of seasons. A summer person myself, I had been pressed into service only because their expected partner had been held late at work. So for me, she was still *this* pig, and as I concentrated on the task at hand—trying to play my part with honor—I realized that my own legs were shaking uncontrollably. When my neighbor signaled that it was all right for me to leave, I snatched up the cigarette lighter that had flown from my pocket and scrambled quickly from the pen.

As the pig breathed her last, we sat on the gunwales of a rowboat abandoned in the tall grass and drank a beer. Then the other two men dragged the dead pig over to a block-and-tackle arrangement in a nearby clearing. Here, where they'd done it many times before, they skinned and cleaned it.

Expertly, they hoisted it, then dipped it in a barrel of steaming water they'd heated earlier. When its whiskers were softened by the heat, they hoisted the pig again and began stripping its hair off. Using a special bell-shaped tool—as well as their hands, brushes, and an old-fashioned straight razor—they gradually revealed the pure white skin beneath the hair. By the time the pig's forequarters were clear, their late-arriving colleague had appeared. Before pitching in, he paused for a moment to appreciate their handiwork. "That's a *beautiful* pig," he pronounced.

And indeed it was. It was also, surprisingly, almost unrelated to the creature which had been fighting for her life only a half hour before. As it—no longer "she"—rotated slowly on its hook, I noticed with mere interest that the shaving had revealed a discreet belly button. And when the men finished cleaning it, and its guts tumbled neatly to the earth, I turned down my share only because I don't much care for pork liver.

Still, later that light, when one of my kids asked if I'd be able to eat the pig, I hesitated, then said, "I don't really know."

The next morning, I woke to the smell of roasting pig. During the week, my neighbor had built a cinder-block barbecue, and by eight in the morning, the pig was slowly rotating three or four feet above a charcoal bed. By the time I staggered out into the midmorning sun, its white skin—liberally coated with lard, oregano, paprika, and black pepper—had become a light gold. While I admired it, other islanders stopped by. Some—able to steal only a few minutes from their work—were "just checking," but others came to help. Summer is the busy season for the island's tradespeople and laborers, and it's only sharing the work (and expenses) that makes special events like pig roasts possible. So, in a ritual that seemed almost as old as the slaughtering of animals, the men and women came and went, bringing their various contributions to the night's feast. And when a temporary emergency arose (the television-antenna motor turning the spit gave out), the neighborhood children, my own among them, took turns rotating the spit by hand.

By five o'clock, the pig was a dark, crusty brown; though it was still a few hours from perfection, people began to arrive in earnest. Folding chairs and tables, along with some platters borrowed from the firehouse, were at the ready, and the first beer keg had already been tapped.

Soon the lawn was filled with cars and pickup trucks. The people who wanted "real" drinks had set their bottles on one of the tables, and everyone else was gathered around the beer tap. From that strategic point, they moved back toward the bushel of raw clams—for every one you ate, you were supposed to open two others—or forward to where the big quahogs were steaming on the charcoal grills. By sunset, we were ready for roast pig.

Two men heaved it from the charcoal pit to an eight-foot carving table, and while it was setting, the trimmings appeared. Coleslaw, baked beans, macaroni salad, mixed greens, potato salad (its maker described herself as having been up to her elbows in potatoes for the previous two days), macaroni and cheese. . . . Plates filled, we began to line up near the carving table.

The hams went first, with much scrap-snatching from the waiting diners and mock threats from the carvers. My neighbor, the butcher and proprietor of the pig, was justifiably proud, and when he held a specially tender morsel out to me on the end of his knife, I took it as my due. It was every bit as good as Charles Lamb had promised.

*   *   *

My memory of the rest of the night is perhaps not as precise as one might wish it to be (I do remember essaying some Irish ballads with the chief of police, not exactly the sort of memory that inspires confidence in one's objectivity), but I recall a number of conversations in which *this* pig roast was compared to all previous pig roasts, and was solemnly adjudged to be best. I was feeling especially lucky to have been at the all-time best right up to the point when someone said, "Hell, the one you're at is *always* best."

I recall as well a conversation on the gunwales of the abandoned boat. It was about the joys—and pains—of pig-raising and pig roasts. And how the island's status as a summer resort has given birth to a host of zoning regulations that make the raising of pigs illegal on much of its land. "Goddamn people come out here from the city," said my neighbor, "and try to tell us how to live."

It's true. To preserve the comfortable fiction that we meat-eaters are unimplicated in the death of the animals we feed on—and, of course, to preserve property values—we would destroy the pig roast and substitute the cocktail party. We should be ashamed of ourselves.

Stocks and Bonds

id all that meowing and rubbing mean Anna loved me? No, it meant she was hungry, and a quick search of the kitchen revealed that she was going to stay that way until someone went out for catfood. The Potato King was at his typewriter, sweating out an essay on St. Simonianism for Mr. Robilotti, and the Woman Warrior was at a meeting. Since the Mad Baker was at that point still living with his mother in New Hampshire, guess who was gonna brave the freezing rain?

Slam. Mutter. Slog. Curse. Splash. Home again. But when I opened the door, a smell I hadn't noticed as it had slowly filled the house made the trip seem almost worthwhile. There is something *comforting* about a stew.

Something basic, too. It's just a matter of simmering two things (edible solid and potable liquid) until they become one. But "basic" is not the same as simple. Traditionally one speaks of letting the ingredients marry, and the metaphor is apt; stews and, er, relationships raise many of the same questions.

Like, for instance, how much of a oneness. Too much, and you're eating undifferentiated sludge; too little, and it's not a stew at all. And what happens when you toss in a few complicating ingredients? Carrots, leeks, wine ... careers, children, spouses. Do they all blend together and enrich each other, or merely clutter things up?

On the kitchen stove, at least, questions of unity and diversity seem manageable. There, the goal is clear: Everything in a stew should taste like itself, but it should also taste like everything else. Which means timing is critical. Take carrots, for instance. If added for the last fifteen or twenty minutes of cooking, carrots will be nicely textured and will absorb a good deal of taste from the stock, but they won't yield enough of their precious bodily fluids to lend flavor to the meat. But carrots added soon enough to let their essence permeate the meat will be bland as baby food by the time they make it to the table.

Of course if you and I were as perfect as we ought to be, we wouldn't have such problems; our stews would always begin from the vegetable-rich stocks we'd carefully stored up in our freezers (and if I had some ham, I'd have ham and eggs if I had some eggs). Also, since stews by definition are supposed to stew for a while, there's a question whether people who work more or less normal hours can ever have a weekday stew.

Fortunately stew is forgiving as well as comforting, and when one piles the logistical problems together, each solves the other; cooking a stew in two stages—preliminary simmering one night, final touches the next—not only leads to a better flavor than a hasty one-night effort, it gives you two nights of wonderful smells.

Still, wonderful smells aren't all there is to life. When this particular stew made its dinner appearance the next night, the Potato King complained that the barley wasn't done enough. Perfection in stews is as subjective as it is in other domestic relationships.

I suppose it's rampant egotism on my part—an image I rather cherish of the rich and complex Estragon—but when for some reason I imagine myself in culinary terms, it is as a stew. This may not be the stew's fault, however, for I suppose whatever foods we pick reflect some highly idealized aspect of our personality. For instance, I once loved a woman who was fond of describing herself as an artichoke. By which she meant, all too explicitly, that if I persevered through her outer leaves and inner prickles, I would find something quite wonderful at bottom. For a time, I believed her. Only after peeling a great many layers with nothing to show for it but tears did I decide she'd been an onion all along. In retrospect, this turns out to have been all right; though it's curious that tears, which one thinks of as obscuring vision, finally cleared it. But I suppose in my stew role, salt—and onions, too—were necessary.

"I am a stew." Hmm, doesn't really have that old Isherwood ring, does it? But that's all right, too; that young man was a rather too refined *pâté* for my taste anyway, though he certainly thought otherwise. Indeed, he saw himself as a mass of colliding solids in a wildly boiling pot. My stew is different. Chunks of my past and present float by at the stately pace of a sea tortoise in an aquarium. Perhaps it's just the continuing exhaustion that follows from having an infant daughter, but everything seems to move more slowly these days; Estragon stew is obviously a thick, peasant sort.

Children, lovers, books, movies, even other dinners simmer together, lending flavor to the stock, connected by it in a way they will never be in the world outside the stew. The Mad Baker—who will, like his brother, soon be off to college—has no memory of the toddler in a light-blue snowsuit and doesn't understand why I worry when he comes home two hours late from a party. Don't I know he's old enough to take care of himself?

Well, no. To me, he trails not so much clouds of glory as strings of misplaced mittens. He's hardly to blame that all those other hims are in the stew along with the nearly adult version who wants to stay out all night, but there they are, and they certainly should be home before two in the morning. Next case.

The stock—which is to say, the me-ness—is by now so flavored by memories that the ingredients can be separated only by the sort of mental exercise that is so abstract as to be unreal, but a junkie friend has just floated by. He had somehow stayed alive past forty when I met him a dozen or so years ago; at the time, he was going through an inadvertent bout of being clean, but he'd been utterly unable to shake the hustler's habits and metaphors. We were discussing a mutual acquaintance one afternoon, and my friend looked at me, his tired face crinkling into laughter, and said, "*Him?* Ma-a-an, he's so dumb he keeps his money in his *wallet*."

That conversation has saved me a few dollars over the years, and I wish I'd repaid them on the spot. He is long gone, a trace flavor in the stock, but if I'd had the wit, I might have played the domestic dozens and responded, "No way. You're so dumb you make your stew with water."

Finally, his systematic erasure of memory killed him. I wasn't surprised; I'd seen him on a street corner a week or so before he OD'd, and there was no there there. Remembering his face as I last saw it, I suspect the empiricist argument that only what we extract from old experiences can be used to flavor new ones is right. But remembering the infant Estragon-Warrior's first smile—fifteen minutes after she was born, when I held her in a warm bath and she opened like a flower—I'm not so sure. But since I—and by now, she—can no longer recover those first dreams, the best we can do is build new ones; it's possible to be a strong stock, and if one is very lucky, an important flavor in someone else's stew.

Or, perhaps, someone else's soup. I basked when the Woman Warrior pronounced my beef stew delicious the other night; the dish is one of her specialties, and for her to applaud mine was a sign of no little esteem. "But," she added, "it's not beef stew. It's beef *soup*."

I stopped basking. You would not think it possible to get several syllables worth of disdain into a simple word like "soup," but she had no difficulty at all. She'd been planning to make that night's dinner, but had relented at the last minute as a favor to me. (There was a reason for this generosity. I'd hoped to spend my Sunday afternoon in front of the TV, suffering as the Giants found yet another way to lose a football game, but had instead been inveigled into shopping—and shopping, and shopping—for baby clothes.) Confronted by this watery (i.e., delicate) sauce instead of a nice substantial (i.e., mucilaginous) gravy, the Woman Warrior felt betrayed.

Prolonged head-to-head discussions of this sort have a way of winding up in divorce court, so I decided to triangulate the conversation. I turned to the Mad Baker—flesh of my flesh, blood of my blood, archetypal victim of a wicked stepmother—for an opinion. "She's right, Dad," he said. Hummph.

What we had here—in addition to a delicious whatever-it-was and a certain amount of ill-will—were two conflicting syllogisms, which I will call, for convenience, "Theirs" and "The True View":

THEIRS:
              (a) Stew is thick,
    but (b) this is not thick.
  Therefore (c) this is not stew.

THE TRUE VIEW:
              (a) Soup is made with little itty-bitty pieces of stuff,
    but (b) this is full of great whomping chunks of meat and vegetables.
  Therefore (c) this is not soup.

Query: Since both conclusions are negative statements, are they truly in opposition? E.g., I say, "It is not raining"; you say, "It is not sunny." If it's snowing, we're both right. This is known as the fallacy of the excluded middle, which it turns out is often committed by those manufacturers of children's clothing who neglect to make a nine-month size, insisting that a baby is either six-months small or twelve-months big. But except that it helps explain why we were in foul moods to begin with, this last example may not be pertinent to an analysis of our disagreement.

Here, we must consider my father and his chisel. Which I, a stripling lad at the time, had used as a screwdriver when I couldn't find (i.e., be bothered to look for?) one. Predictably, I chipped the blade, rendering the chisel useless and my father angry. He waved the damaged implement back and forth before me. "This is a chisel. It is not a screwdriver. It has never been a screwdriver. It is a chisel."

My father, you will have gathered from this, was in Platonic terms an idealist. *Chisel* and *screwdriver* were for him exclusive ideal forms; the tools in his workshop were one thing or the other, depending on the extent to which they partook of either chiselness or screwdriverness.

I, by contrast, was a realist (in a Platonic sense only. Any child with a prudent notion of reality would not have used one of my father's chisels as a screwdriver). I had driven a screw with the goddamn thing; therefore it *was* a screwdriver (I did have enough ordinary-language realism to forbear pointing this out to him).

So it seemed to me that the opposition's soup/stew distinction was based on a false ideal. No doubt they were disappointed that reality, in the form of my stew, did not conform to their ideal, and their disappointment grieved me. Deeply. But my regret could not blind me to the necessity of making logical distinctions. Consider split pea "soup." Thick, right? Thicker than this by a long shot. Would you call it "stew"? No, not on your life. If you let it cook down to the approximate density of a Frisbee, it would still not become a stew. Ditto mushroom and barley.

And how about, to take another tack, classic *boeuf bourguignon?* Its sauce is no thicker than this. Do you call it a soup? No. And what about *S'chee*, the Russian cabbage-and-beef concoction? What about that, huh?

"You know," said the Woman Warrior sweetly, "there's no

need to shout. When I heat it up for lunch tomorrow, I'll thicken it. That's all." And she did. And I tasted it. And it was better.

~~~~~~~~~

BEEF SOUP-STEW

The important events in making a beef stew happen early. In shopping, do not buy packaged supermarket stew meat. The pieces are too small; if you cook them long enough to flavor the stock, they get tough. Buy a chunk of round—or, if near a kosher butcher, some kalechel—and cut it yourself into cubes a couple of inches square (1½ lbs. will serve 4 nicely). Brown these, in a thin layer of fat, in a very hot, heavy pan.

Not so fast there, buddy. DO NOT RUSH THE BROWNING. Do only a few pieces at a time (if the pan gets too crowded, it cools off and the meat begins to steam, which gives gray instead of brown), removing them as they're done. When the last pieces are thoroughly browned on all sides, add the chunks you've already done and a cup or so of boiling water (or, if you've planned ahead, that nice beef stock you've been keeping in the freezer).

From here on in, you're home free. Add about 4 more cups of cold water and a generous glass of red wine, together with 1 large, peeled onion, 1 celery rib, a couple of carrots, a bunch of parsley, a few peppercorns, a little (you can add more later) salt, and maybe some bay leaves or a little thyme. Let simmer (not boil) for an hour or so, then remove those vegetables, and add cut-up chunks of whatever veg you want in your soup-stew. When they are tender, taste for seasoning, and serve.

Oh yeah. Many people prefer a thicker sauce. You can achieve this either by flouring the meat before you brown it or by cooking 3 or 4 tablespoons of flour in an equal amount of butter over low heat until it begins to color (about 5 minutes), and adding it to the pot 10 minutes before serving.

CARBONNADE DE BOEUF À LA FLAMANDE

This is one of those instinctively wrong notions—like stuffing money into your pocket instead of your nice wallet—that works out better than you think. It has too many onions, for one thing, and the stock is made with beer, for another. But it's delicious.

1. Slice 8 medium onions fairly thin, and sauté them—very slowly—in a half-stick of butter until they brown (about 20 minutes).

2. While this is going on, brown 3 lbs. chuck—cut in large cubes—in a very thin layer of lard or butter. Do only a few pieces at a time (too many will cool the pan and get gray instead of brown), transferring them to a heavy, coverable casserole as they're done.

3. When the meat is done, turn off the pan and add 3 tablespoons flour to it, stirring to absorb all the fat (if all the flour isn't absorbed, add a bit more butter). Cook this paste even slower than the onions, until it turns a deep, deep brown.

4. Pour into it 2 bottles dark beer and 1½ cups beef stock. Let it boil for a few minutes, stirring it enthusiastically, then add a teaspoon of sugar, a tablespoon of wine vinegar, 2 chopped garlic cloves, a bunch of Italian parsley, and a goodly shake of dried thyme.

5. Pour this sauce, and the onions, into the casserole along with the meat. Let it come to a boil on top of the stove, add a generous amount of salt, then cover the pot and cook it in a 325-degree oven for about 2 hours. To serve, simply remove the tired bunch of parsley and sprinkle some fresh leaves into the casserole. This is especially nice with broad, buttered noodles. Serves 6.

Next Week: Cockles

I am not now, nor have I ever been, a fisherman. I tried it a few times as a kid, and always wound up bored and unsuccessful. I have since been persuaded once or twice to abandon my solidly conceived prejudice; the major improvement over my youthful experience is that now in addition to getting bored, I can get drunk. If God had wanted me to spend my afternoons dangling bait in the water, he wouldn't have invented fish markets.

Crabbing, however, was (and is) something else—simple, almost instantly gratifying, and fun. For equipment, I needed only a crab net (something like a basketball hoop with the net sewn shut, attached to a five- or six-foot pole), some heavy string with bits of nicely rotting fish tied to it, and a bucket to hold the crabs. Sometimes I'd lean off the edge of a dock, but more often work from the rocks that dot the Long Island Sound shore. Ten minutes after I'd dropped the line, one or more blue-clawed crabs were pulling at the fish. Catching them was simply a matter of bringing in the line slowly enough to leave their dinner undisturbed, and easing the net under them. In an hour, you could catch a lot of crabs.

Oddly, we didn't eat crab very often. They were a pain in the neck to clean, and the reward didn't seem worth the effort. Most of the time, the crab bucket got dumped back into the water, though if there was a particularly ugly or lively specimen I might carry it down to the beach and use it to scare girls.

Still, eating crab was at least a theoretical possibility. Yet in all my scrambles over the seaweed-slick rocks, the notion that I might pick up a handful of mussels for dinner never even occurred to me. They were everywhere, great chains of them clinging to the seaweed, but my repugnant little gang of boys used them only as missiles in our amphibious war games. When my parents told me the French actually ate them, I was shocked. No wonder it took Americans to win the war.

Now, of course, it's getting hard to find a restaurant that doesn't serve mussels. They come cold, marinated, or with a sauce ravigote, or hot, in the mode of steamed clams. Either way, they are delicious, and—perhaps even more important at a time when restaurants are unblushingly charging five dollars for a half dozen shrimp—dirt cheap. Order steamed mussels and you get an overflowing bowlful.

With all that, I have nonetheless found it difficult to treat mussels with due seriousness. I don't know whether the attitude is a hangover from my youth or a reaction to the casual prodigality with which restaurants ladle them out, but there it is. This summer has begun a change, however. Though the Woman Warrior had been working on me for a while—as an Upstater, she had none of the shore-dweller's disdain for mussels—the tipping point came one evening when the younger Tasteless One arrived home from his work as a dishwasher at La Terrasse, a tony local eatery. Since they feed him—and since I feel that parents should occasionally show polite interest in their children—I asked what he'd had for lunch. "*Moules,*" he said.

And how were they? "Delicious. You should do them sometime. They're easy to make."

I felt, I guess, a little like James Mill must have when young John Stuart began formulating original counterarguments, but I am not about to look a gifted child in his increasingly discerning mouth. And though there is certainly nothing wrong with a plate of plump, pink steamed mussels just waiting to be dipped in lemon butter, my apology for a misspent youth is a soup so elegant that striped bass plays second fiddle in it.

~~~~~~~~~

ABSURDLY LUXURIOUS MUSSEL SOUP

1. Make a stock by melting 1 stick of butter in a heavy skillet, and then adding to it 3 cups chicken broth, 1 tablespoon chopped fresh parsley, ½ tablespoon chopped fresh tarragon, a dash of curry powder, ½ cup dry white wine, 3 tablespoons lemon juice, 2 large (or 3 small) fish heads, and a large bunch of seaweed (both the latter items are generally available at fish markets, though you may have to ask). Simmer for half an hour, strain, and return to the (rinsed) pot.

2. Add to the pot 1 lb. unpeeled new potatoes, cut in smallish cubes, and a ½-lb. chunk of striped bass. Simmer for about 15 minutes.

3. As the potatoes and bass are cooking, beard (i.e., pull the seaweed off) and scrub 2 qts. of mussels. Put the cleaned mussels in a covered pot and cook them over high heat just until they have opened (about 3 minutes). Remove the mussels from their shells and reserve.

4. When the potatoes are cooked, reach into the pot with a fork and break up the bass into small flakes. Add the cooked mussels, and when the pot has returned to the boil, add ½ cup of heavy cream.

5. Serve very hot, with a crusty bread and cold, dry white wine. Serves 6.

If Seafood Falls in the Forest...

U nlike most Most Unforgettable Characters, this colorful, crusty New Englander was talking violence. "Cherry bombs," he said. "You just wait till you see the bubbles, then drop one down. It deafens 'em."

He flapped the door of a lobster pot back and forth. "Skin divers. It's bad enough they go in there at all, but they leave the door open behind them. They steal what you got and don't even give you a chance to catch any more. Cherry bombs."

Apparently taking the depth-charge notion one step further, he continued, "You know, a lot of people are taking shots." This seemed to me to carry crustiness beyond the pale, and despite a sneaky belief that lobster is metaphorically worth killing (or at least deafening) for, my face must have registered dismay at the reality. "It's true," he said, malevolently waving a sharply pointed brass instrument. "You put this hook, right here, behind the eyes, and if the body doesn't reach to this end here, you can't take the lobster. It's a shot."

Recovering from my misunderstanding of the Cape Ann accent, I considered the lobster. Especially the short lobster. I suppose there is some point below which lobster is too small to eat, but I've yet to find it. As a child, I grew up among bootlegged shorts that my father (much to the scorn of my Uncle Arthur, who felt that any lobster smaller than King Kong was hardly worth cracking open) had managed to score. He was as excited by these devious purchases as my kids are by the odd ounce of primo Colombian that comes their way. Illegality is a sauce. I didn't care. Big lobster, small lobster . . . all the same to me. Annoying, mostly. Not worth the effort. Too many nights, I slid a lobster around on my plate without ever getting to taste any. By the time some butter-dripping adult finally took pity on me and removed the meat from its crustaceous armor, I'd grown cranky and lost my appetite. No matter what size the beast, one thing was clear: lobster was for grownups.

Now, more or less grown up, I no longer see as through a glass darkly, and the virtues of lobster have become shiningly self-evident. The lobsters themselves, however, have become neither self-opening nor self-cooking, and though with each advance in age and hand-eye coordination I've become more adept at dismembering lobster once it's reached my plate, cooking them still makes me queasy.

It's not that I go through the *Annie Hall* shtick or anything, it's just that the moments when I plunge a living creature into a pot of boiling water are not among my happiest. I do it all right—you know, big fleas have little fleas and all that (they actually have, I just read, a parasitical ringworm that eventually castrates them; Mother Nature is pretty crusty herself)—but not without discomfort, for it's all too obvious that lobsters don't much like being boiled to death.

And I don't believe for a minute the easy reassurance offered by James Beard (in his *Fish Cookery*) that "lobsters are most insensitive creatures." I know any number of insensitive creatures—I'm scheduled to have drinks with one this afternoon—but their insensitivity alone wouldn't excuse my knocking them off. (If it did, Jean Harris would be a free woman today.)

Beard, by the way, subsequently hedges. "They wriggle," he notes, and suggests it "would be helpful if more American fish dealers would adopt the French custom of trussing the beasts with string when they sell them." *Helpful*?? To whom? Much more of this and we'll find ourselves talking about protective reaction strikes. If anything it would be "helpful" if fish dealers went the other way and sold lobsters with their claws unpegged. This way, lobster eaters would damn well earn their pleasure. Helpful would also be if fish dealers came up with an easy way to open clams. Mostly, I think, because it's wicked hot today, I've been having elaborate fantasies about the perfect hotweather lunch: two dozen freshly opened Little Necks and a couple bottles of ice-cold lager. None of that red "cocktail" sauce on 'em either, just lemon and coarse black pepper. Yum.

Or, alternatively, yecch. Which is the way many people react to the thought of a raw clam. I say "the thought" because I think it is the *idea* more than the reality that gets them. After all, unlike lobsters, the clams don't *do* anything. And you don't have to *do* anything to a clam. If these people could bring themselves to try that first one, the second—and seven hundredth—would slip right down with no trouble.

In that sense, clams are different from lobster. (Yeah, I know, "Clams got legs! Clams got legs!") But *B.C.* notwithstanding, there's not much a clam can do to overcome prejudice. To the eye of a beholder not already committed clamwise, a raw clam is *not* beautiful, and no amount of trussing at the fish market will help. That the identical shimmering clam can look so different to people gives one new respect for the power of ideas, for it is the clam in our head—delicious, ambrosial, food-for-the-gods vs. slimy and, er, clammy—that determines what the clam on our plate looks like. And, finally, how it tastes.

I wonder if Bishop Berkeley liked raw clams?

~~~~~~~

BOILED LOBSTER

There are other ways to cook lobster, but broiling has always seemed to me pointless and steaming inescapably cruel. Boiling is close to foolproof. Set a very large pot of heavily salted water to a rolling boil and plunge the lobsters in, head-first, as rapidly as possible. Let them cook 8 minutes for the first pound, 6 for the next, and 4 for each subsequent pound. Do not crowd the pot; if necessary, cook the lobsters in batches. Serve, traditionally, accompanied by bowls of lemony melted butter—or, for a change, spike the butter with lime juice and a jolt of Tabasco.

CLAMS OREGANATE

In general, the best way to cook clams is as little as possible. (I speak here neither of soft clams, a.k.a. steamers, which one obviously steams, nor of the granddaddy chowder clams, which have to be thoroughly cooked before they become chewable.) A cherrystone or Little Neck left too long on the fire turns into something that in taste and texture is indistinguishable from an eraser. Erasers are eaten only by small children and people who order fried clams at Howard Johnson's.

One exceedingly nice thing to do with clams is to prepare them in a more or less Italian manner, coating them with a topping and popping them briefly under a very hot broiler. For 3 dozen clams, you should start out with about 1½ sticks of butter ("about" because I don't know how big your clams are) and 2 large cloves of minced garlic. Using a fork, cream the butter and garlic together, and gradually add bread crumbs until the mixture no longer sticks stubbornly to the side of the bowl. Then add about 4 tablespoons chopped, fresh parsley (preferably the flat-leafed variety) and an equal amount of grated Romano cheese. Cover each clam-half completely with the mixture and broil until the topping becomes brown and crispy (3 or 4 minutes should do the job nicely). If you have been genuinely fanatical in covering the clams completely, they will remain moist and juicy beneath the crust. Serve with lots of lemon wedges. Yum again—and no yecchs at all.

Supply-Side Chicken

*H*ave you noticed there aren't any real good songs about chickens? There are some okay ones—"Dixie Chicken" and "C-H-I-C-K-E-N" come to mind—but none that do for the bird what Norman Greenbaum did for eggplant. That is to say, mythologize, magnify, even ennoble.... The closest analogy in pop culture is Big Bird, and chicken he never wert.

This is unfair. (I know, I know . . . life is unfair. And with heating oil a buck and a quarter a gallon, who can worry about chickens' egos. Blah, blah, blah. Listen, buddy, I would rather worry about chickens than Three Mile Island any day. Besides, who first told us the sky was falling?) It's also mysterious. True, chicken is unassuming, but your eggplant isn't exactly pushy. Chicken is also American in a Norman Rockwelly way that eggplant will never be; a politician running on a platform of an eggplant in every pot would be well advised to seek a new media adviser.

Nevertheless, despite Frank Perdue's ubiquitous (and hardly altruistic) efforts to resurrect roasters, the whole chicken seems increasingly to be a creature of the past. The Potato King was gainfully employed in the meat department of a large supermarket a couple of summers ago, and to hear him tell it, his daily work consisted of cleverly cutting up chickens and packaging them so that at the checkout counter the sum of their parts would equal considerably more than the whole. But such non-Euclidian chicken isn't just a triumph of merchandising, or even of "convenience," for behind the array of tidy packages on the meat counter stands the hard-core, irreducible reality of the chicken; no matter how you slice it, it has two breasts and two legs. And though industrialists like Mr. Perdue are all too evidently doing their best to render the dark meat as flavorless and texturally uninteresting as the light, there remains a difference that is instantly detectable by people who claim to prefer white meat. Thus chicken in its natural, unreassembled state has a better than even chance of throwing any group of four diners into turmoil. The four poultry-eaters nearest and dearest to me, for instance, divide into three white meat and one dark—something that would probably bother me a lot more if I were among the gang of three. As it is, I just sort of sit there, my chin all greasy with thigh juice, and watch them squabble.

Still, though there's a certain amount of sadistic pleasure to be gained from watching the intergenerational pull-and-tug, there's also an element of risk. Sometimes, in the manner praised warmly by Marx and tepidly by John Paul II, the oppressed classes realize that their struggle is not with each other but with the piggy dark-meat lover who purchased a whole chicken in the first place. Faced with this tri-pronged assault (and by the way, "Mother and Child Reunion" does not count as a song about chickens and eggs), I cower and make all sorts of promises to reform.

These aren't false at the time I offer them—though the vision of a whole chicken, crisply brown, shiny and smooth as an eggplant, is hard to deny—but due to circumstances beyond my, or the chicken's control, they turn out to be hard to keep. Mostly, these circumstances are financial. They concentrate in that hateful period that follows hard upon the ritual chorus of "Happy New Year." All that remains of Christmas (except for the mysteriously reappearing pine needles that seem to *breed* in our dining-room floor) is a series of increasingly urgent Mailgrams from the nice folks at American Express ("Dear Mr. Estragon/We value your membership of fourteen years, but what the fuck?/ Cordially"). Second-semester tuitions are due, the Youngest Member has cleverly outgrown her snowsuit, fuel-oil prices are doing their annual dance upward, and there are six more weeks until the first hint of a March bleat. And so, always, we are on a food budget.

Actually, what we're on is a tighter food budget than usual; from time to time, that dreaded document has a little give to it, but never during the post-Christmas slump. This year is typical; over the past couple of weeks, we've had baked beans, Yankee bean soup, lentil soup, and too many pastas to mention; next week's menus include lima bean and barley soup and Spaghetti Carbonara (without the cream).

I fart a lot, but that's the least of my worries. Last night I woke with an erection and realized I'd been having a vividly erotic dream about a rib roast; if this goes on much longer, I'll be afraid to go to the supermarket. ("New York, AP—Four policemen were injured today attempting to drag a hamburger-smeared Yahoo from the meat case at the Newkirk Avenue, Brooklyn, Food City . . .")

These are the times, in short, when any promises made about chickens are off. True, chicken isn't "real" meat, but neither is it dried beans, and it's almost always on special at one neighborhood market or another. When chicken becomes virtually one's only meat, its great drawback—the comparative flavorlessness of American mass-produced birds—becomes its chief advantage, for there's an almost infinite number of ways to disguise it. Rather like one of John le Carré's intrepid professionals, it blends unobtrusively into various exotic international settings, seeming quite at ease in the local culture. When you get right down to it, chicken is the next best thing to Shmoo.

Am I going on too much? Sounding the eentsiest bit like I'm actually trying to convince myself how swell chicken is? I sound that way to me, but maybe I'm wrong. Maybe I look forward to chicken just as much as I claim to ("I think I can, I think I can," puffed the little engine), but I somehow doubt it. I would make a lousy Christian Scientist.

On the other hand, we're having vegetable curry tonight. If I think enough about vegetable curry—not as one dish among many during an Indian meal, but as, in its entirety, my dinner—chicken does seem pretty good. Still, maybe it's not any specific in the new lean, mean Estragon budget that bothers me, but the fact of restriction. I'm actually very fond of the Woman Warrior's lima bean, mushroom, and barley soup; it's the *having* to have it that makes it a trial.

Maybe I could pretend that the whole food budget is just a lark, a little game we jaded jet-setters play when the more obvious pleasures of Palm Springs begin to fade. "Let's have a round of Poor Folks," we say, and laughing gaily through the night, we put aside darling Binky's caviar blini and begin instead to dice salt pork for the Yankee bean soup. What good times we have!

Fat chance.

～～～～～

CHICKEN MORE-OR-LESS GRANDE-MÈRE

(A 4-lb. chicken will quite nicely serve 4 people who divide either 3-to-1 or 2-to-2 on the light/dark question. At 4-to-0 think twice about this dish.)

1. Heat 4 tablespoons butter and 2 tablespoons peanut oil along with 2 garlic cloves in a heavy, coverable Dutch oven.

2. In the cavity of a chicken, place ½ lemon stuck with 4 cloves, 1 bay leaf, and 1 stick of celery. When the garlic has begun to color, remove it from the fat and add the chicken, breast side down. When the breast has nicely browned (about 3 minutes or so), turn the chicken on its side to brown the thigh and leg; continue the process until the chicken is pretty.

3. Add to the pot 4 large (6 medium, 8 small, etc.) new potatoes chopped into chunks about 1 inch square. Stir them quickly to coat in the liquid, sprinkle with salt and pepper, reduce the

heat and cover the pot. Cook for about a half hour, turning the chicken and stirring the potatoes every 10 or so minutes.

4. When the chicken is almost done (test by inserting a fork into the joint between the thigh and the leg; the juice should run faintly pink, not bloody; if it's absolutely clear, take the chicken out and keep it warm in a slow oven), add 1 lb. fresh shelled peas or 1 package thawed frozen peas. Recover, and cook only until the peas are tender.

5. Arrange the peas and potatoes, all mixed together, around the chicken on a serving platter, and prepare a simple sauce by pouring off all but 2 tablespoons of the cooking liquid, and adding to the pot 1 cup dry white wine in which 2 tablespoons of cornstarch have been dissolved. Heat this, scraping all the crispy brown from the pot into the mixture, until the sauce thickens (about 2 minutes).

———————

CHICKEN & WINTER VEGETABLES

Grousing aside (and a nice roast grouse would be just fine, thanks), we did a clean-out-the-refrigerator chicken the other night that turned out to be so good the Mad Baker astonished us by coming back for seconds on vegetables. Since the veg included parsnips, this was a minor miracle; since I wanted some more myself, I decided the Practical Joker in the Sky has a lousy sense of humor.

1. Quarter a lemon and tuck it inside the cavity of a whole, medium-sized (2½-to-3-lb.) chicken. Melt a couple of tablespoons of butter and an equal amount of olive oil in a heavy Dutch oven and brown the chicken (drying the skin with paper towels and sprinkling it with salt and pepper before putting it in the pan) over medium-high heat. This is pretty tedious work—it takes 15 or 20 minutes—but really makes the beast look and taste better. Helpful hint: If you use wooden spoons to turn it, you'll be less likely to break the skin and let those precious bodily fluids leak out.

2. When the chicken is brown, toss in 6 peeled shallots, reduce the heat to low, and cover the pan. The chicken will be
done in about 40 minutes (test it by poking the joint between
the thigh and the body with a fork; if the liquid runs clear, it's
done).

3. Cut 3 or 4 carrots into a julienne, ditto parsnips. Parboil
them until they are almost—but not quite—done. If you've been
compulsive enough about cutting them, this shouldn't take
more than 3 minutes. When the chicken is done, uncover the
pot, turn the heat high, and toss them in among the shallots
along with a half-handful of chopped fresh dill. Stir them around
until they're all coated with the chicken, butter, and oil mixture
and have just barely started to fleck with color. I usually serve
this right out of the pot, but if you've a mind to, you can make a
pretty showy platter out of it.

4. Don't forget to save that carcass. Along with the various
innards, it will make a fine stock for those goddamn dried-bean
soups.

Table Talk

he words, internally illustrating Grimm's law, always came out "Basda Vazool" and sounded to me like an exclamation of the sort offered by amateur carpenters immediately after smashing their thumbs with a hammer. Milder than "cocksucker" (which, when the second syllable is accented, is more expletive than characterization), but a good deal stronger than "drat." It was the sort of thing I thought Italian-American cabdrivers—a raffish crowd by Larchmont standards—said a lot. When I was feeling unusually daring (and figured my mother wasn't listening), I imitated them. I think I was in college before I learned I wasn't talking dirty.

Some insults do not translate well. When I was a good deal older, a gun-toting Puerto Rican friend used to refer to his political rivals as *chuletas,* a term which sounded venomous indeed. It was when he chucked my then-young children under their chins and addressed them with the same word, albeit in a different tone, that I asked him what it meant. "Pork chops," he said.

Well, all right, I guess. Children are allowed to be pork chops—or little lambkins, for that matter. But I don't think you could call them turkeys and expect doting parents to look pleased. And if you address them as cabbages, you should probably be French.

Speaking of turkey, as I was just a moment ago, did you know there once existed—though Wentworth and Flexner sternly annotate it as "never common"—a phrase, "To have a turkey on your back"? It meant to be drunk and is an altogether more satisfying image than the later junkie-monkey. It is possible, having a monkey on your back, to be mysterious; to have a turkey flapping and gobbling behind you is to be inescapably ridiculous.

So much for turkeys, you think. Not so fast, buddy. I've been leading up to a story here. True story. Goes back to those happy days before there was a New York City fiscal crisis. Seems that the Housing Administrator, one Jason Nathan, wanted to spend a little bit of the cash that then appeared to be plentiful to put up some buildings. Nathan wrote a memo to Mayor Lindsay complaining that the city's Budget Bureau was preventing him from building houses by sitting on paperwork. Lindsay, fond of houses, apparently got on phone to Budget Director and said, "What means?" Budget Director Frederick O'R. Hayes (nice man) waxeth apoplectic. Denies that Budget Bureau *ever* delays paperwork (big lie, but that's another story). Fires off memo to Nathan. Begins "You Turkey! You pious Turkey! You pious, sanctimonious Turkey!" and goes on to dispute Nathan's claim. Copies leak out. Nathan unable to attend cabinet meetings without faint sound of gobbling behind him. Soon leaves city government.

Hayes also is responsible for the classic budget-cutting memorandum on the city's chaplain service that suggested (though admitting the difficulty of quantifying output) a squad of praying laymen might be more cost-efficient. Though bureaucrats as a breed are notoriously unamusing, Budget Bureau types often break the mold. Perhaps it's gallows humor.

Remember Al Kahn, Jimmy Carter's inflation fighter? When he was forbidden by the White House staff to say "depression" in public, he went before a national governors' convention and gave a speech during which he regularly used the word "banana" in place of the interdicted term. This ruse, though clever, fooled nobody and is rumored to have made the White House image-makers a little edgy (though not, I suppose, as much as they would have been if he'd used "peanut"). This was jus' fine for the image boys—who didn't want to go back to pumping gas in Atlanta—but I don't think Kahn was fair to bananas. Languagewise, the banana is in big trouble already; if you call someone a peach, it's considered a compliment, but if you call them bananas, they look at you funny. (Consider also the following sequence: lips like cherries, cheeks like apples, nose like a banana. See what I mean? Not to mention banana republics.)

And another thing. Do you know anyone who's ever actually slipped on a banana peel? Of course not. I will tell you something about banana peels, which is that it is damned hard to slip on one. One afternoon when I was hiding from my typewriter, I spent about a half hour trying to slip on a banana peel, and all I did was mush up the kitchen floor so bad I had to mop it (which was all right because it gave me a swell reason not to write; the banana is my friend). You want to fall down and bust your head sometime, you should drop by after the boys have eaten grapes.

But what, you ask, does this have to do with the frozen food business? A considerable amount, actually, but it'll be a long slow curve. It starts out with depression. Not the kind which dared not speak its name in Washington, but the good ol' postholiday slump. All animals can be sad after whatever they want; I'm annually done in by Christmas. And no wonder. Not only is the season to be jolly officially past, but there are a good eight or ten weeks left before the first asparagus. Since I'm usually pretty sick of broccoli and winter squash by the end of December, this means an endless vista of frozen veg.

You would think, ill winds and so on, that while the rest of us were struggling and cursing over our Master Charge bills and frozen Italian vegetables, Mr. Birdseye would be down there turning handsprings in the streets of the financial district. But not so. The thought of that other kind of depression has even the Jolly Green Giant blue. You see, in their ceaseless efforts to carry us through the season of no fresh vegetables worth the name (and to turn a tidy profit on our deprivation), the frozen food folk have allowed themselves to become "upscale." Indeed, by gussying up their string beans with almonds and their cauliflower with cheese sauce, they have deliberately made themselves so. Now, unless all those supply-siders who've taken over the federal image franchise are less transcendently full of shit than they appear to be, the frozen food moguls are in trouble plenty.

They regard this as unfair. "Upscale," after all, is where the action is; a frill here, a foofaraw there, and the next thing you know, you're getting a buck a pop for a package of "continental-style" vegetables. But with the current (and apparently humorless) crop of budget-cutters having decided to risk a banana, downscale is the coming thing, and Wall Street is shopping around for "defensive" companies—the kind one industry-watcher describes as those "whose products are traded down *to*, not down *from*." In other words, goodbye frozen spinach soufflé, hello canned kale.

And hello, presumably, dried beans. And you can certainly imagine my disappointment when I eventually learned that what I'd thought was a colorful Italian insult turned out to be a plate of macaroni and beans—than which there are few products more defensive. I suspect it was my chagrin that more than any other factor accounted for my avoiding the dish over the next several years. I overcame my prejudice only when Alfredo Viazzi (of Trattoria d'Alfredo, *inter alia*) suggested I try a bowl one cold lunchtime. I did (if Viazzi offered a bowl of pigs, snails, and puppy dog's tails, it would probably be delicious), and immediately regretted my self-imposed abstinence.

But somehow, though I've cheerfully ripped off dozens of dishes from Viazzi, I never got around to this one. Besides, when the Woman Warrior entered my life, she held the dried-bean franchise. So it was with a certain amount of dismay that I noticed myself, one January evening a couple of years ago, preparing my first pot of *pasta e fagioli*.

This event came to pass because in between the making of the weekly menus and the execution of same, we had a nine-pound baby girl, and the Woman Warrior was temporarily excused from kitchen duties. My version of the dish had elements of the thrown-together, but it tasted just fine. And though I suspect it probably had more to do with the arrival of the Youngest Member than with the success of my first *pasta e fagioli,* I suffered no post-Christmas banana that year.

<hr />

PASTA E FAGIOLI

Carefully rinse 1 lb. red beans (preferably pinto, but kidneys are all right) and put them in a large, heavy stew pot. Pour in enough chicken stock to come an inch or two over the beans; cover and cook until tender (about 90 minutes); add water if they seem to be getting too dry. Add 1 lb. coarsely chopped carrots; 2 large, chopped red onions; a half bunch of chopped Italian parsley; 1 large can Italian tomatoes with their juices; a few tablespoons of tomato paste; ½ cup good olive oil, 1 cup dry red wine; a few shakes wine vinegar, a tablespoon or so dried red pepper flakes, and ½ teaspoon cinnamon. Cook, stirring occasionally, for another half hour. At that point, remove the cover, and add 1 lb. short, tubular pasta. Serve, when the pasta is tender, with lots of freshly grated Parmesan. Serves 8, comfortably.

Dessert Is in the Mail

The Mad Baker must have been only three or four years old—young enough at any rate to be forbidden to make his own breakfast—the morning his smiling face testified that he had broken the rule. Fixing him with my best steely gaze (there was, after all, some danger in unsupervised cooking), I asked, "Did you have anything to eat this morning?"

"No," he said, lying like a trooper.

"Then how come there's chocolate all over your face?"

"There is?"

"You fuckin' well bet there is. And for your information, there's also some on your nose. Now let's try it again: Did you have anything to eat this morning?"

He paused—obviously auditioning several other tales for plausibility—before finally assuming a transparently phony expression of dawning recognition. "Oh, *right,*" he said, somehow restraining himself from an aw-shucks snap of the fingers, "I had a Bosco sandwich, but I forgot."

Lots of people lie about what they eat. I suspect that if I habitually knocked back Bosco sandwiches, I'd think twice about admitting it. I mean, how many times have you heard someone claim he or she doesn't "particularly like" sweets, although you've seen them—repeatedly, lunch after lunch—launching with the greatest gusto into Café Loup's lethally rich chocolate cake?

As a rule, adults' lies tend in the direction of understatement; it seems that only children vastly overinflate reports of their intake. And usually, too, dessert is the proximate occasion of sin. It is as though a fondness for chocolate were as socially debilitating as a fondness for sodomizing squirrels.

Not to imply, not for a moment, that sex doesn't inspire its share of fibbing. I knew a married man so besotted with lust for his secretary that he would race home from work, eat a dutiful dinner with wife and family, then take his dog "out for a walk" of some three or four hours' duration, the perambulatory part of which consisted solely of the brief journey to and from his secretary's apartment. Unlikely as it may seem to sophisticates like thee and me, this ruse was actually successful for a time and might indeed still be going on if he had not forgotten one night to bring the dog along as he raced randily out the door. Result: tears, divorce, awesome cash settlements.

Most lies about food don't turn out so badly. Sometimes, demanding my full share of whatever pitiful scraps have finally made it to the table, I neglect to mention the amount the cook is forced to consume in "tasting" (heh, heh). In this case, the only real damage seems to be to my own waistline. And I have a friend whose devious eating has actually enriched the world by adding a word to its stock.

Dinni is both her name and her gift. "To dinni (var. dinny): to make disappear the leftovers as unostentatiously as possible; p. dinnied, pp. dinnying. 'Aha, you knave, I caught you dinnying the rhubarb pie.' " It is the "as unostentatiously as possible" that is the definition's heart. Any gorilla, faced with a table of five people, each of whom has had one slice of pie and might well enjoy a fair share of the remainder, could simply shovel a heap of pie onto his or her plate and dare anyone to take it away. But only your true dinnier, maintaining a lively conversation all the while, can whittle the pie down to nothing without ever being seen bringing fork to mouth. Such virtuoso performances have their drawbacks (viz., a lack of seconds on pie during that bleak between-marriages period when she and her husband made me part of their family), but I forgive them for the gift of the word.

Oh, *right.* I probably should have mentioned that to distinguish it from dinnying, the name given what I eventually got caught doing in the kitchen before dinner is "picky-pokey." But I forgot.

CHICKEN FRICASSEE WITH TARRAGON

You would think, wouldn't you, that large pieces of heavily sauced chicken would be virtually impervious to dinnying. But you would be wrong. Never will I forget the genuine amazement I felt when I began to dish out seconds of this dish and found, beneath the sauce, nothing but clean-picked bones. This version serves four honest people.

1. Halve and slice 3 medium-large onions and sauté them, very slowly, in a half-stick of butter until they begin to color. Add ½ lb. mushrooms (whole if they're small, halved or quartered if large) and continue cooking for about 5 minutes. Remove the vegetables and set them aside.

2. Add another ½ stick of butter and a couple tablespoons of vegetable oil to the pan and brown, 2 or 3 pieces at a time, a chicken cut in the conventional 8 parts, and dredged with flour, to which salt and pepper have been added.

3. When the last pieces are done, remove them and pour off any extra fat remaining in the pan. Deglaze the crispy bits on the bottom with about 3 cups winy chicken stock, and when the liquid has come to a boil, reduce it to a simmer, add the chicken parts, veg, and a generous tablespoon of dried tarragon leaves, and cover. In about a half hour, add 1 cup heavy cream, and when the sauce has returned to the edge of a boil, serve. Over rice.

4. If Dinni's there, don't leave the pot anywhere near her.

Where Do Correct Ideas Come From?

"*M*ower? Mower? Baby wants some mower?" It was late spring, and I was—there is no other word for it—*chirping*. A simple word like "more" had taken on two syllables pitched like the bob-white's call. "OOOOpen the mouth. That's right. OOOOpen the mouth." Obedient more to nature than to me, the Youngest Member opened up for another spoonful of rice cereal. I could have been auditioning for a grade-school science film, except that it always used to be Mommy Bird dropping food into those yawning beaklets. Daddy Bird was presumably at his office.

Not this daddy. Nosirree. The typewriter clacking away in the background wasn't his. This daddy was on his front porch, chirping dementedly and wondering if the next scene would find him on the lawn, hopping around and trying to pick up a worm with his mouth. Yecch.

In some ways, a diet of worms would have been an aesthetic improvement over the Youngest Member's first solid foods. I mean, you rarely see a baby bird with worm running down its tiny chin, but there was *always* one or another variety of gump on the Youngest Member's. A spoonful of cereal ("OOOOpen up") went in, and a large percentage of it immediately ("God-*damn*") came out. Mealtimes were something of an ("Nooooo,

175

baby. Doooon't grab the spoon. Let Daddy put the spoon in your mouth. Here it is. Niiice rice cereal. OOOOpen the mouth. We OOOOpen the— God*damn*") adversary procedure. Nice baby might have a malleable mind, but also a grip of steel. She's considerably more sophisticated these days—munches Cheerios and bay scallops—and seems almost as delighted to have stopped eating baby food as I was to stop feeding it to her. She never showed any passionate dislike for the stuff—though she had her doubts about carrots—but she found food in her hands, in her hair, or tucked inside her diapers more interesting than in her mouth. I can't say I blame her. Infants' rice cereal, even (or perhaps especially) mixed with soybean formula is about as jazzy as Cardinal Newman's prose. Maybe we should have tried something a little *oomphier*.

I ate bugs as a child, and apparently found them tasty. I don't remember the experience, but my mother recalls hearing the young Estragon babbling away in the back yard, "Go 'way bug. Go 'way or I eat you." She instructed me not to eat bugs and when I grew silent, considered the matter closed. But a few minutes later she heard, "Go 'way, bug. Go 'way or I eat you, too." Adverbially prompted, she arrived in time to rescue the second ant, still quite lively, from my mouth; the first was history.

So why are some foods appealing and others not? Restaurateurs have long known that the brain is as important an organ of taste as the tongue; that's why they hire decorators. On the domestic front, rabbit is rabbit, venison is venison, and both in their different ways are delicious. But not if one has Beatrix Potter or Bambi too much in mind; ideas are powerful.

Remember "droodles"? The simple pencil sketch was unintelligible until one was told what it was. Then, almost magically, it was *of course* a ship arriving just too late to save a drowning witch (or a nudist bending over to retrieve a collar button, or whatever). An analogous process happens when we're presented with food; ideas—organizing principles, expectations—determine our reaction to it.

Consider my conversation with a neighbor child who toddled by one afternoon to announce that our cat was bad. I demurred (I think Anna's pretty swell) and pressed for an explanation. "Bad cat," he said firmly. "Bad cat kill the bird." His reportage was unassailable. To see Anna hunting is to understand what Tennyson meant by "red in tooth and claw." I suggested, however, that his judgment was faulty: "She's not a bad cat. She *eats* the birds."

"Yick."

"Eating birds isn't bad," I continued, remorseless as Perry Mason. "*You* eat birds."

Look of absolute horror: "Do not."

"Sure you do," I said pleasantly. "You eat chicken, right? When your mommy fixes it for you?"

"Yes," doubtfully.

"Well, chicken is a bird."

"Is *not*."

The conversation ended there—what was I going to say? is *too?*—and he went away to wreak God knows what havoc at his family dinner table. Or maybe just to shut up and eat his chicken. The connection between the crispy brown thing on his plate and those bloody feathers on the lawn may have been too tenuous for belief. I sort of hope so; I didn't want to spoil his supper but to defend our cat.

Still, Anna's honor notwithstanding, I wouldn't offend the neighbor child by serving him one of those tiny whole birds the Chinese crunch down head and all. Remind a kid that chicken was alive and there's a nasty scene, but let him think they make it in factories and everything is fine.

I'm probably the same way myself. For all I know, an ant I ate for dinner tomorrow would be every bit as tasty as the one I ate years ago. But I'm not going to make the experiment. Unlike the Youngest Member, I've been corrupted by experience.

But if all that's true, how come she never liked carrots? The flavor of even the strained variety doesn't seem inherently repugnant, and the texture, God knows, is indistinguishable from other baby foods. The color is the same as strained squash, which she ate like a trouper; was she born with an innate idea about carrots? Bertrand Russell would have been disappointed in her. The concept disappoints me as well, for despite the evidence the Potato King daily puts before me, I have a firm belief that tastes can be educated and the range of acceptable experiences broadened. This is sometimes uphill going; faced with Brussels sprouts, for example, many adults make wrinkly faces that would do a teen-ager proud. And Brussels sprouts are by no means the worst offenders. The merest hint of anchovy can send folks spinning back into their high chairs—where they sit, slack-jawed and drooling, with bits of anchovy running down their pouty little chins.

This has always seemed an overreaction. Anchovies may not be everybody's dish of tea, but they needn't be anathematized. Yet there they are—harmless little fish, important chiefly to the economy of Portugal and to larger fish—causing discord and contumely at dinner tables all over America. A little missionary work is obviously in order.

Fortunately, anchovies are easy to disguise, and the wise anchovyphile—recognizing the unreasoning passion of the anti-anchovy brigade—does not attempt frontal assault. Face it, when a mere glimpse of crossed filets decorating the egg yolk atop a Caesar salad can reduce an anchovyphobe to puling infancy, attempts to substitute a tube of anchovy paste for the menthol Crest are foredoomed.

No, defenders of the fish must operate with subtlety (or, as some would testily suggest, sneakiness), camouflaging it and, when successful, resisting the temptation to jump up at the end of dinner and shout, "Aha! You know what *you* just ate?"

Announcements of this sort can turn mealtimes into an unpleasant clash of wills and are likely to result in the anchovyphobe's slowing up your dessert by holding forkfuls of the main course up to the light. Besides, it's unnecessary. The missionary spirit is satisfied simply by knowing that from thesis and antithesis, synthesis can emerge. The aim, after all, isn't the dictatorship of the anchovyphile but the withering away of distaste. Which terrible pun leads us neatly to the story of the Marxist Economist's pizza. Or, at any rate it *would* lead us there if I didn't have this little digression in mind, but we'll get there soon enough. (Linear thinking is deceptive anyway. I was taught ontology by a wonderfully devious Jesuit, whose syllogistic march was so neatly arranged into ranks, files, and bagpipe bands that it took me several years to realize the parade route was a circle.) Point is that foods do move us around in time, and the effects don't always have to be as disastrous as anchovies putting grown-ups in jeopardy of colic and diaper rash. Other dishes bring us back to a time in childhood that is within our memories' reach.

The cooking may be simple or complex—a bowl of oatmeal on a cold February morning or a platter of fresh cinnamon doughnuts—but they have in common, I think, that they were prepared for us when we were too young to fend for ourselves. Faced with such fare, the crustiest curmudgeon will become magically pliable, for such dishes imply love.

(I'm secretly convinced that a scenario like this was responsible for ol' Jimmy Carter's otherwise inexplicable success with Begin and Sadat at Camp David: "Oooh, *latkes!*" exclaimed Menachem one morning. Bursting with contentment and goodwill, he left his table and found Anwar sitting dewy-eyed over a bowl of figs and cream. They embraced on the spot and agreed that, from now on, they would play nicely and share their toys.)

Of course the culinary time trip isn't always wonderful; every now and then the memory isn't of unconditional love but of pimples, unpredictable body odors, and gargantuan clumsiness. Which is another way of saying that I don't like pizza.

My sons and their friends do—to the extent that I sometimes think "going out for a pizza" is their code-word way of protecting me from the bizarre rituals actually practiced in their teen-age covens. But this may be a projection; when I used to tell my parents I was going for pizza, the pie *an sich* was usually the furthest thing from my mind. I was more interested in the hanging out.

For a number of years, however, I failed to make this distinction. I liked drinking beer and arguing sports so much that I also thought I liked pizza. It wasn't till I turned eighteen and could hang out in bars that I discovered a burned tongue and stained shirt weren't part of male bonding.

Or of courting. My basic junior high school date was a movie and a pizza. The movie part was okay—you could hold hands and didn't have to talk—but the pizza was genuinely perverse. Maybe not for everyone (there certainly seemed to be ninth-grade sophisticates who didn't think girls were scary), but for me. There is no way to be Cool when you've got a stringy gob of hot mozzarella trailing from your mouth. None.

In the long run this may not have been so bad. Pizza is an equal-opportunity destroyer, and girls suffered the same tortures as boys. Thus we learned not only something of equality but the perhaps more important (then) lesson that one could make an asshole of oneself and still be lovable. In the short run, however, eating pizza under such sweaty-palmed circumstances wasn't much fun. I left pizza and adolescence with equal relief.

My emotions were therefore exceedingly mixed when my friend the Marxist Economist announced one summer that he was going to make pizza for dinner. And that he was inviting five people from the house next door to share it. Swell, I thought, I can eat a greasily messy food that I don't like in front of company. Still, the kids were lyrical over the pizza prospect, and it was his turn to cook. I prepared myself to suffer graciously.

The first clue that I might be girding myself unnecessarily arrived over lunch, when the Marxist Economist revealed his topping plans and asked for any amendments. He was designing five pies, each with two different toppings; one half, in deference to the prejudices of my older son, was to be plain, but the rest were big-league stuff. When he got to the half that featured steamed mussels, blanched bacon, and sage, I felt resignation changing to greed.

By late afternoon, with the smell of tomato sauce penetrating every cranny of the house, I was in a fine gustatory frenzy. The folks from next door had come up the hill and were pitching in, so I didn't have much to do but admire the various ingredients spread about the kitchen. In addition to bunches of herbs from the garden, there were bowls of chopped onion, sautéed potato slices, parboiled artichoke hearts, julienned zucchini, asparagus tips, et cetera, ad infinitum, and so forth.

My memory has blurred by now, and besides, even with judicious trading, I didn't get to taste every possible variation, but I *think* my favorite was the sautéed asparagus, mushroom, and parsley combo (though the zucchini, onion, and oregano was a worthy rival). None of them, however, not even the plain cheese, tasted anything like pizza. They couldn't have, because I loved them, and I don't like pizza at all.

MASHED BANANA

1. Purchase a single overripe banana. Reserve.
2. When baby cries, race to bring banana into her view, announcing "Banana. Ba Na Na."
3. Peel the banana, discarding the tough exterior skin.
4. Put the banana on a plate and mash the bejeezus out of it with a fork. When it is the texture of good sour cream (and the smell, oddly, of new varnish), stop mashing.
5. Serve *instantly*. Serves one 6-month-old, generously.

~~~~~~~~~

UNTARTAR STEAK

1½ lbs. hamburger
1 medium-large yellow onion, chopped
3 tablespoons capers
2 tablespoons prepared Dijon mustard
2 to 3 good shakes Tabasco sauce
6 anchovy filets, mashed with a fork
2 egg yolks
3 tablespoons chopped fresh parsley

Fearlessly mungle all the ingredients together and shape them into 4 thick rounds. Let come to room temperature (about one hour) and broil quickly.

Simple buttered broccoli, garlic bread, and a no-holds-barred red wine (a Rhone, Chianti, or—if you're splurging—a good Burgundy) complete a sneakily satisfying dinner for 4.

~~~~~~~~~

SAUCE FOR PROUD PIZZA TO THE PEOPLE
(enough for 2 pies, plus some useful surplus)

1. Cut 2 lbs. tomatoes in half, and cook them, covered, over medium heat for 10 minutes.

2. Add ⅔ cup *each* chopped carrot, celery, and onions, a medium bunch of coarsely chopped fresh basil leaves, 2 teaspoons salt, and ¼ teaspoon sugar. Simmer uncovered for a half hour.

3. Run the whole thing through a blender and return it to the pan. Add 3 teaspoons finely chopped rosemary, sautéed for a minute in 2 tablespoons olive oil; pour in a scant ½ cup olive oil, and simmer, uncovered, until the sauce is nicely thick (about 15 minutes). Taste, and add more salt if you need it. (Two cups of canned plum tomatoes may be substituted, and the recipe begun at step 2.)

The Usual
Suspects

Pâté de Shmoo and Fish Perloo

*N*obody in the comic strips eats well. One expects Shoe and the Perfesser to spend all that time at Roz's amazing diner; they're journalists with no family life to speak of. But even Dagwood, that paragon of sitcom domesticity, isn't such hot stuff in the food department. He never really looks at his breakfast (always either rushing or reading that goddamn paper), and half the time he forgets his lunch. Which sends *him* off to a bizarro diner. And after his daily bout with Mr. Dithers, he either goes home (where the expression on his face when he smells dinner does not inspire confidence in Blondie's cooking), or out to a snooty restaurant where he is bullied by the waiter. If it weren't for those sandwiches, he'd starve. I think he's even eating *them* less, these days. And not just because the joke is wearing thin, either; he's been knocking over the postman for years. Maybe he's not feeling well. I worry about Dagwood.

Though with all his troubles he's better off than Charlie Brown. Only one ever eats in that strip is Snoopy (and Woodstock, but he eats like a bird and doesn't count). Mary Worth eats like a bird, too. Or a rabbit maybe. "Just let me finish this cabbage leaf, darling, and I'll come right over and save that troubled marriage of yours." Beetle Bailey eats Army food.

Andy Capp is different. You never actually *see* him eating (mostly because he'd have to move his cigarette), but I know he's knocking back fish and chips or bangers and mash whenever we're not looking. Al Capp, in one of his few signs of decency, used to feed his characters pretty regularly. Mammy Yokum was always whipping up po'k chops dipped in tea for dinner—and it was Capp who gave us the Shmoo.

Remember Shmoos? Lovable little animals who regenerated instantly and whose happiness consisted in sacrificing themselves to human whim. Broiled, they tasted like steak; fried, like chicken; boiled, like ham. They also (somehow, the process remained obscure) gave milk. And soda. I wish I had a Shmoo.

I wish Winnie Winkle had a Shmoo. She's been through a lot lately and she deserves a break. She doesn't eat enough, either. You look at her and she's always setting the table, or cooking for the family, or giving her order to a waiter. But she never brings fork to mouth. Her life is one long dinner interruptus.

Brenda Starr, by the way, is not giving that baby of hers enough solid food. I think of this as Brenda's job because what does Basil know from food. He eats black orchids, fer chrissake.

Food is not a problem for Superman. Neither is anything else. I do not wish I had a Superman. But I was always kinda fond of Mary Marvel. I don't remember what she ate.

I don't remember about Krazy Kat, either. I have a feeling that he/she did not go in much for things of the flesh, and that even his/her passion for Ignatz Mouse was largely of a spiritual nature. I will not speak of Mickey and Minnie.

Wiley Coyote doesn't eat much, of course, but that's his shtick. Ditto Sylvester the cat (though I, for one, would love to see him do that supercilious canary in once and for all). They suffer worser even than Winnie Winkle.

The folks in Doonesbury don't eat much either. They drink and smoke and stuff, but they rarely sit down and pack it in. Except at Thanksgiving maybe. But we know what they eat off-stage. Cucumber sandwiches for Lacey Davenport, beansprouts and avocado and Yodels for Zonk—the usual. And in a way I'm glad that Trudeau has drawn the veil of modesty over Duke's diet. Some things, like the water in Dagwood's bath, are better left opaque.

I sure do miss Pogo, though. And those wonderful fish perloos.

Weasels Ripped My Cheese

*P*rune juice, for instance, is not inherently funny. I mean, if you looked at (sniffed, tasted) a glass, you would not burst into gales of somewhat snarky laughter. Nevertheless, let Johnny Carson but lift an eyebrow about Ed McMahon's waker-upper, and there we are, living laugh-tracks. Some foods are like that.

Still, prune juice (and beans, cf. campfire farting in *Blazing Saddles*) is humorous only output-wise; if you don't believe it, show someone a handful of dried pea beans and see if they think it's a laff riot. Okay?? Okay.

Rutabagas are something else. They aren't particularly amusing in appearance, but their name is just weird enough to push the giggle button (e.g., suppose George Washington had been named O. Leo Lahey; would distinguished museums be squabbling over his portrait?). A rose by certain other names *wouldn't* smell the same. Skunk cabbage, as it happens, has a particularly graceful leaf, but it would take an intrepid sonneteer indeed to launch into "My love is like a green, green skunk cabbage."

Limburger.

I was just testing. But on the basis of several absurdly unscientific surveys, Limburger seems to be good for a laugh (or smirk). Not because of its name or associations, but because it smells. In fact, Limburger seems amusing even to people who've never actually gone nose-to-nose with one. It has this rep, see.

I myself find Limburger more tragic than hilarious—it's rather like someone who so desperately wants to be popular that he/she goes to inordinate lengths to cultivate a degree of repulsiveness that will both guarantee and cushion rejection. "Neurotic," I guess, would be better than "tragic."

But mozzarella isn't even neurotic (it is certainly, God knows, not tragic). Cold, it is almost preternaturally inoffensive—less bouncy than a Spaldeen, more nourishing than an eraser, more boring than either. Yet Jackie Gleason used to get laughs just by mentioning it. Admittedly, that was in a more innocent day, before mozzarella became as American as pizza pie, and maybe it just sounded bizarre that anybody would willingly eat something that had so many z's and l's in it. Maybe.

At any rate, it was probably that lingering memory of Gleason's routine that made me giggle when I ran across a *Wall Street Journal* piece chronicling the intricate connections between the mozzarella biz and the you-know-who. The you-know-who were very big in the news, what with the speculation that Aldeana "Jimmy the Weasel" Fratianno was speaking unkindly ("singing like a canary") of his former associates in the you-know-what, but amid all the lurid tales of crunching kneecaps and Atlantic City real-estate deals, the notion of cornering the mozzarella market might have burst full-blown from the mind of Milo Minderbinder.

But here we are—in hardcover, now, for *WSJ* reporter Jonathan Kwitney subsequently expanded his researches in a book called *Vicious Circles*—faced with a prudently unnamed official of the Kraft Cheese Company remarking that his firm eschewed the mozzarella trade because "Kraft was afraid criminal elements might burn Kraft trucks, or commit other acts of violence if Kraft tried to compete."

This is heavy stuff, and one cannot read Kwitney's elegantly documented reports of the way Vermont dairy farmers were systematically bankrupted without feeling outraged, but then one is forced to face the hard question, viz., "Do I *want* to eat Kraft's mozzarella?" Or am I indeed glad that there is some force, however malign, that is holding them off?

This does not demonstrate good citizenship, I know, but I kinda think I am. Sort of in the same way that I am willing to put up with the exceedingly erratic schedule at a certain Brooklyn restaurant that is located suspiciously near the corner where the car used in a recent murder was found (by "erratic" I mean that when a certain table in the rear fills up with certain people, the waiter will interrupt you in the midst of whatever course you're eating to announce that the restaurant is closed now). The food there is quite good, but even I think it odd that the police, looking up from the getaway car and seeing all these men in black suits and white-on-white shirts heading for dinner, told reporters that the car was found "only 11 blocks from a large Rastafarian community." There is no justice in Babylon.

~~~~~~~~

MOZZARELLA IN CAROZZA

1. For each person to be fed, take 2 pieces of old white bread, put a ¼-inch slice of mozzarella between them, and trim the bread to the shape of the cheese.

2. Sprinkle a little oregano on the cheese, and cut each sandwich in half.

3. Heat an inch of vegetable oil in a heavy skillet; as it's getting hot, dip the edges of each sandwich first in milk, then in breadcrumbs.

4. Dunk the sealed triangles into beaten eggs (as with french toast) and cook them briefly in the hot oil (turning delicately, if need be, with two forks).

5. Serve either as is or with a sauce of melted butter, crushed anchovies, and garlic. Grilled cheese was never like this.

6. If the waiter tells you the restaurant is closed, don't ask why.

Food and Drug Administration

The slate-gray sky had gone dark outside the coffee shop's grimy windows. Snow swirled in the circles of greasy yellow light from the ancient street lamps, and even over the babble of voices, I could hear a mean wind whistling up off the river. Inside the restaurant, it was even more threatening.

There were one or two obvious Americans—I imagined their traveler's checks and passports safety-pinned to their underclothes—but this was the nerve center of Eastern Europe, and the Americans were never really welcomed. Even in the disguise I'd spent years perfecting, I was never sure what I'd find when I walked in through these doors—and never certain that I'd walk out.

Today was the worst it had been. The agents—mostly Ukrainians who'd first collaborated with the Nazis, then trimmed their sails to follow the new ideological winds—seemed more boisterous and self-confident than usual. Bustling through the narrow aisles, they shoved each other good-naturedly, and masculine laughter erupted from under the fur hats that circled the large corner table.

But the laughter strangled quickly to a halt, and during these odd, oily patches of silence, the agents stared at us. As I pushed pirogen around my plate, I would become aware of the spies' scrutiny and look up to see if I could pin one's gaze, but each time I did, the spurious machinery of normal café life wheezed and clanked back into gear. As they played out their masquerade, we did our best to fall inconspicuously into the coffee house rhythms.

The woman across the table, my partner in this adventure, was still beautiful, but she was clearly frightened. Her face was paler than I'd remembered it, and she seemed unable to lift her eyes from the bowl of cabbage soup steaming before her. "Doin' okay?" I asked, trying out a grin for effect.

"The soup," she said. "It's *raging*. There are huge tidal waves crossing it . . . back and forth, back and forth. Soon, if I don't watch it all the time, it will all leap out of the bowl and go 'splat' on the floor." She paused, then continued, "I would have told you earlier, but the last time I looked, you had five heads, and I didn't think I could trust someone who had five heads."

Well, shit, I mean I'd figured out what all those foreign agents were doing in a Lower East Side luncheonette (Hitchcock's *Torn Curtain* on late-night TV a couple of days earlier), but it was disconcerting to learn that my five heads had scared my friend. Ever since then I've tried to lay in a supply of manageable food before starting an acid trip, but sometimes food that seems easy enough to handle when you're straight becomes a little complex when the stove is alternately melting into the wall and swelling up to refrigerator-size. Another friend—a painter—once baked a whole fish toward the end of a trip. He had surrounded it with vegetables, and before he put it into his oven, he called us all out into the kitchen to admire it. "A Chagall, a Chagall," he chortled. About fifteen minutes later, his somewhat worried voice called me. "I need a little help," he said. "The Chagall has cooked into a Bosch." Turns out that whole fish snarls when baked.

I have never had anything like the classic bad trip—indeed, on acid I find things remarkably jolly. I once watched a good friend chased along a slippery pitched roof by a swarm of angry wasps who'd been disturbed by his carpentry and roared with laughter as he nearly plunged to his death (he was not amused)—but I do have this problem. I get hungry before I get straight. *Really* hungry. Hungry enough to eat four White Castle hamburgers, which, given how they taste, is very hungry indeed. (Remind me to tell you sometime about the interesting street theater at the Washington Avenue White Castle in Albany.) So far, the most comforting thing I've found (a discovery made—later, alas—by the cabbage soup woman) is a giant slab of fresh bread liberally slathered with your own sweet butter. Which is exceedingly exciting to make, under the circumstances.

HOME-MADE SWEET BUTTER

The nice thing about this is it's hard to fuck up. Basically, because it's already a mistake, sort of (you remember what happens to whipped cream if you forget about it in the blender. Becomes butter, right? Right).

For enough butter to completely pig out two very stoned people, pour a pint of fresh (*not* ultra-pasteurized) heavy cream into the blender. Cover it (that part is important, all things considered), and push one of the little buttons. Let it run. And run. Push the stop button. (Here, you might actually want to unplug the blender. You don't really need to, but think how much *safer* you'll feel.) Pour off the thin liquid, and scrape the butter onto a plate. Carrot bread is nice.

Bad Company

*T*o begin with, I suppose I should explain how they happened to be in the refrigerator at all. The Rich's Frozen Eclairs, I mean.

It was the snow's fault. A month ago, the season's first real snow had found us severely unprepared, and when the governor closed the banks so we couldn't cash a check and go shopping even when a few stores struggled open, we endured a weekend of cuisine that can most kindly be described as functional. There are only so many ways you can skin a leftover.

We got through it all right—thanks mostly to the Woman Warrior's residual hippie way with mysterious dried things—but I remember that weekend as Dr. Johnson did *Paradise Lost:* "None ever wished it longer than it is." Next time, I vowed, things would be different.

And so they were. I had fortuitously done a big weekend shop, so even before the Potato King made the first of his (many) hopeful announcements that he was *sure* there'd be no school Monday, the refrigerator was in pretty good shape. The confirmation he so devoutly wished came late, however, and he'd made it up to Flatbush Avenue before a subway clerk gave him the news. He bounded cheerfully home, and his loving father immediately handed him money and ordered him back out into the blizzard. "Buy things," I said, and kept typing.

My instructions were actually a bit more precise, involving both fresh meat and some lurid recapitulations of what we'd eaten the last time it snowed. He returned shortly, proud as any Arctic explorer, with a huge brown bag. Parental pride overflowed: What a splendid lad, I thought. On inspection, however, the bag was revealed to contain Coca-Cola, milk, and potatoes. Never send an adolescent on a human's errand.

Which is why, typing finished and manuscript dauntlessly delivered to *The Voice,* I found myself thumping through the nearly deserted aisles of a supermarket at two in the afternoon. I'd successfully gathered six thick pork chops and some prudential mysterious dried things when the lights began blinking on and off. "Everybody out," the manager ordered. "We're closing."

I was at that moment standing in front of the frozen food case, and I guess I just lost my head. In the last moment before I was herded to the checkout counter, I snatched up a package of Rich's Frozen Eclairs. Even at that time, I suspected this was a mistake, but I remembered the mere nourishment of the previous storm all too well. I wanted something *frivolous* in the house.

The ritual unpacking included a considerable number of skeptical comments about this particular purchase, and I was more or less forced to defend it. "You can't tell," I said. "They might turn out to be good. It says they're filled with Bavarian cream, right?"

Now "Bavarian" is not a synonym for "ersatz." Some national adjectives clearly are—if one orders Romanian tenderloin at the luncheonette, one expects not tenderloin but diaphragm. That's fair. Others are ethnic slurs, the culinary equivalent of Polish jokes: Scotch woodcock, English monkey, Welsh rabbit (the perverse and growing substitution of "rarebit" is a bit of Welshophiliac *Volksetymologie*). But "Bavarian cream" is the real thing. At least by me.

Though not, apparently, by the Rich Products Corporation of Buffalo, New York. Close examination of the ingredients listed on the package of "Four Bavarian Cream Filled Eclairs"—which examination occurred promptly after one taste of the nasty stuff—revealed that while they included eggs, they had not a trace of either milk or cream. The absence of the latter was, in the curious mind of Mr. Rich, evidently more than made up for by "vegetable fat, corn syrup solids, starch, salt, modified cellulose gums, artificial flavors, lecithin, polysorbate 60, artificial colors, polyglycerol esters of fatty acids, agar," and "ammonium bicarbonate."

This is, let me tell you, *not* Bavarian cream. Fannie Farmer—as anyone who has had occasion to use her cookbook can testify— was no reckless hedonist, but her recipe for a modest amount of Bavarian cream includes both a cup and a quarter of milk and a half pint of heavy cream. *That* is Bavarian cream. The terms *mean* something. I suppose if ol' Rich wants to emulate the makers of Hostess Twinkies and call his eclair-filling Bavarian "creme," he has a right to do so. That spelling would at least give fair warning—though not, perhaps, as fair as a skull-and-crossbones.

Do I go on too much? I think not. I know it sounds like the worst sort of cultural puritanism, but my prejudice is aesthetic rather than ideological. I'm not one of your basic nuts-and-berries types (you ever look at the people shopping in health-food stores? They're all sort of gray-green and sickly), and no one as fond as I am of salt cod can seriously oppose preservatives. It's just that more often than not, the real tastes better than its imitations.

Take hot chocolate. Along about the ass-end of winter, when the cold has become boring rather than bracing, hot chocolate is as spiritually warming as a crackling fire. Which is to say that the sense of well-being one receives from a wbfp or a steaming mug of cocoa cannot be measured by BTUs alone.

Provided, of course, that one is drinking the real thing. The various "instant" cocoas throw off about as much warmth as a fireplace's photograph (and taste, I suspect, not a whole lot better than the chemicals used to develop it). Even assuming that the mixes use real chocolate—and not the cotton derivatives favored by the many manufacturers who are trying to prove Mencken's maxim about the taste of the American public—the end result is oversweet and thin. The real stuff is creamy.

(A *Voice* editor, an otherwise reasonable woman, here demanded that I say something about Swiss Miss [and other mixes that contain dried milk]. She asked this because she kept a package of the stuff in her refrigerator "for emergencies," and wanted to see this practice approved in print. Not on your life. It is preferable to be keeping a vat of cyanide-laced Kool-Aid around, but not by much. It's also better than Nestlé's Quik. By about the same margin. Editors are too powerful.)

It also takes maybe a hot three minutes longer to make than the brown water, and the real reason most restaurants lay the "instant" on their customers is cost. To make real hot chocolate, you have to use milk (and maybe a dab of heavy cream at the end), but a cup of Instant Yucko requires only a packet of chemicals and some hot water. Since water is considerably cheaper than milk, about the only way you can get real hot chocolate outside your own house is to posh it up and hit Rumpelmayer's or the Peacock.

This is by no means a bad thing to do (and by no means an inexpensive one, either), but it has an exceedingly significant drawback: viz., when you've finished your cocoa and are feeling all cuddly and cozy, you have to go back outside and get on the IRT. This, like getting up and going home in the middle of the night, changes the experience for the worse.

The difficulty with such midnight bed changes is partly moral—the element of deceit is determinedly unromantic—but aesthetic as well; at 3 a.m., already a little worried about explaining one's earlier absence, one is likely to pass up the juice-and-coffee jolt that marks a true morning. At best, there is a quick slug from the ready-mixed sitting in the fridge, then into the streets. This is not right; even under the best circumstances, waking is burden enough to deserve substantial cushioning, and real juice is less an indulgence than a medicine.

But the undoubted restorative aspects of freshly squeezed juice don't make it some sugar-coated pill; it is good all the way through. At least that's what I think, though a recent television commercial reminded me—as they all too often do—that my taste is a long way from universal acceptance. There I was, totally caught up in the last game of the NBA championships, when the Great American Cretinous Commercial Couple suddenly appeared on my TV screen. This time they were wearing what I understand the trade calls "patio garments," so we should know they were from Florida. In case we weren't sure, however, they told us. Repeatedly. They also told us they had a grapefruit tree in their back yard. At first, I thought this—together with their patio wear and overall cleanliness—was simply to indicate they weren't welfare sluggards, but it turned out to be their credential as juice experts. According to them, they can't taste any difference between a glass of frozen concentrate and the juice from their very own tree.

Deep down, I suspect that the money offered them by the frozen-juice folk was not without influence in the numbing of their wee Floridian taste buds, but there are other possibilities as well:

1. They don't have a tree at all but are only Showing Off;
2. They really *can't* taste any difference—perhaps because they both came straight home to drink their juice after extensive dental work and the Novocain hadn't yet worn off; or
3. They hate to squeeze the real stuff so much they haven't had any in years and have forgotten what it tastes like.

Of the three (though they had very nice teeth indeed), the third seems most likely. Until recently I'd always found squeezing the stuff to be Not Quite Worth It. It was easier to walk a couple of blocks out of my way and stop at the B&H—where, in addition to the fresh-squoze, I received both a splendid breakfast and some stylized verbal abuse from the countermen—than to work myself into a desperate sweat wrestling with a citrus fruit. But for Christmas I got an electric juicer. Though I loved it from the first, I was afraid it might be merely an infatuation (my past is littered with abandoned Erector sets and junior wizard kits). But the electric juicer shows no tendency to hide under the bed and gather dust. If anything it gets rather more use than I'd expected; what comes out of it tastes so good that I've been sipping on an occasional evening juice.

Indeed, the only reason I hesitate to recommend it universally is its expense. Not so much the initial capital outlay (it cost about the same as a good blender), but the purchase of fruit. True, having it around means that we drink more, and bigger, glasses of juice, but even if our intake had remained unchanged, we would never get as much yield as the commercial processors. One reason is that they stomp the bejeezus out of their fruit— thus providing, with the added oils from the skins, the acrid bitterness that is the hallmark of their product. And then there's the quality of the fruit itself. There are good grapefruit and bad grapefruit; the good ones cost more.

The really bad ones, of course, never make it to the market. They're bought up by the commercial processors and chunked into the smash-em-up along with good ones, old boots, and whatever else is available. So maybe the trouble with that nice Florida couple is simply their lack of horticultural skill, and they should use the money they earned from their commercial to buy a juicer and some nice grapefruit. They can always use the extra freezer space to store their packages of frozen eclairs.

REAL COCOA

1. Take off your boots, wriggle your toes around, and remind yourself that you don't have to go out again today.

2. For each cup, put 1 teaspoon cocoa (Droste's is wonderful,

Van Houten's very good, and Hershey's okay), 2 teaspoons sugar, and 3 or 4 tablespoons water in a heavy pot.

3. Stir it into a paste and bring to a boil over very high heat. When it's boiling so hard the bubbles start climbing the side of the pot, pour in cold milk (1 cup per cup) and heat until it's on the edge of boiling again.

4. Pour into mugs and add, if you feel like it, something nice. A little whipped cream, maybe. Or some Amaretto. Or a couple drops of vanilla extract. Creme de Menthe is nice, too. [My newspaper editor recommends Kahlua.]

Chacun à Son Goo

*A*t midnight, a nurse's aide removed the bedside water pitcher and replaced it with a sign reading NOTHING BY MOUTH. In the morning, a blue-smocked technician appeared, shaved a patch of hair from my forearm, inserted a needle in a vein, and quite efficiently hooked me up to a food supply.

It was not, at least at first, as unpleasant as one might have expected. It didn't precisely *hurt,* and the occasional backup of blood along the tube provided a colorful diversion. Besides, when you get right down to it, I wasn't missing much; New York Hospital is a helluva fine place, but you would not mistake it for Lutèce.

Or even Nedick's. Hospital food is bland by definition, but the good folk laboring in the kitchens at NYH carry a bad thing too far. One of the menus offered around during the day when I was dining intravenously included something described as "Cheese Dream with Syrup." I do not know exactly what went into said dream—in fact, I prefer not to think about the possibilities—but its very existence was enough to make me appreciate the virtues of a steady infusion of glucose and water. (Maybe it was on the menu as a sort of test. You know, anybody who checked it off was sent immediately to brain surgery. But this is unlikely. The thought probably results from the excellent pain killers with which I am still dosed. Bring on the Joshua Light Show.)

The point is that sign: NOTHING BY MOUTH. Here I was, in no discernible pain (that came *after* the operation, thank you), my ability to wander about the halls hindered only by my rolling armamentarium of bottles, adequately nourished, and *haunted* by thoughts of food. I didn't need anything, but I wanted.

Oh, how I wanted. And, oh, alas, *what* I wanted. Did Estragon the well-known gourmet think of the splendid salmon mousse Berry's turns out? No, he did not. Did he, perhaps, think of the miraculously crusty semolina bread baked by Brooklyn's Guarino Brothers? Not on your life. He focused on the hot-dog man who hangs out on the corner of 68th and York. It was the last real food I'd seen on the way in. Two interns had been standing near his wagon, wantonly feasting on sauerkraut-laden franks. I remembered them. I smelled the unmistakable pungency of the memory. Like St. Anthony in the desert, I fought to subdue the vision. "Come on," I said to myself, "if you're going to torture yourself, why don't you do it *right?* Think about the stuffed zucchini at Alfredo's."

I succeeded, briefly. Then the circuits got crossed and I tuned into Reese's Peanut Butter Cups. And there, dear friends, I stayed. For ten and a half hours, until they mercifully shot me full of sedatives and wheeled me off to the operating room, I was in the perpetual presence of a peanut-butter cup. I tried to recapture the hot-dog man, but he'd gone off duty. I tried sex in its various combinations and permutations. I tried "Suppose the operation goes wrong and I die." But even these dependable standbys failed absolutely. The crinkly texture of the orange wrapper, the sensuous peeling of the softer brown paper inside, and then the marvel of the thing itself.

Over and over again, hour after hour, I explored the classic peanut-butter-cup alternatives: Does one pop the whole thing in at once and let it melt or bite it smartly in two. You would be surprised how thoroughly one can occupy oneself with this question—especially when experimental solutions are forbidden. Anesthesia came as a relief.

When I awoke the next morning, the fantasy and the tubes were gone. I had triumphed. Not only was I knocking back a poached egg on toast, but I had managed to keep my shame secret. Still, when the Woman Warrior went shopping on my first day home, she somehow knew to bring home a great thumping box of peanut-butter cups.

I wonder what else I babbled about.

Myself and Others

"**G**reat" dinner parties—the sort that achieve hardcover permanence in someone's memoirs—don't come around that often (among other things, you have to assemble a bunch of guests who are given to autobiography), but pleasant ones are the rule rather than the exception. You would, however, not think this true if you spent any time reading the panicky "how-to" guides that litter the pages of traditional women's magazines. And even of *The New York Times* (though I say "even" as a hopeless nostalgiast; the *Times*'s special sections are spiritually indistinguishable from Bloomingdale's catalog). Though there are so many truly wonderful examples that choosing a favorite is arduous, I still recall with fondness an illustration from a Sunday *Times* "Entertaining" section that dealt with a Mexican dinner. In the foreground, a squeaky-clean mom and daughter rested manicured hands on their unsullied cutting board and grinned loopily toward the camera; behind them, edges blurred in frantic activity, bustled a black woman identified only as their "cook-housekeeper." I was sort of hoping to turn the page and see the faithful retainer coating her employers with nacho cheese and running them under the broiler until they bubbled nicely, but no such luck. The *Times* and I differ about what's entertaining.

Nevertheless, it's true that some folks do get all in a swivet when it comes to giving a party, and perhaps they found the *Times*'s hints reassuring. I doubt it though; it seems to me that the last thing people with servants need is still more reassurance. It's the rest of us—unable to follow a recipe for *civet de lapin* that begins "First, have Mellors catch your rabbit"—who occasionally need to be reminded not to worry.

For instance, I once lived with a government whiz kid famous equally for her analytical prowess and her *boeuf à la mode* who was completely unwomaned to discover that the glittering company she had laboriously scheduled into her Chinatown loft included a pair of vegetarians. The flutter seemed to me unnecessary; sooner or later, if you are in the habit of feeding your friends, you will come across someone who eschews what you chomp. But it ain't no big deal.

Still, it often seems enough to stir panic in the hostly heart and dither in the hostly behavior. Both, given a little courtesy on each side of the host–guest equation, are unnecessary. The first requirement is fair warning from the guest. For some reason (related, I suspect, to a lack of red meat in the diet) many vegetarians are keenly alert to the possibility of hostly dither. But in their efforts to avoid such discombobulation, they err on the side of discretion. Having remained silent about their preferences, they take their place at table and do their quiet best to avoid fleshly offerings. This does not work.

I suppose, actually, it might work if you were given to having forty or so friends at your intimate dinners. In smaller groups, however, even the most graceful and well-intentioned vegetarian is likely to be noticed eating string beans while everybody else is lacing into the tournedos Rossini. This casts what is known as a pall. The host rushes from the table to forage around the dank bottom of the refrigerator in search of alfalfa sprouts, and the other guests—unless they have managed to insulate themselves quite thoroughly from various guilts—find their pleasure vanishing. Even if the vegetarian guest says nothing at all to inspire it, they will feel piggy. And gross. And disgusting. This is not a happy situation.

Once fair warning is given, however, it's the host's move. Groans, sighs, and suggestions that the whole thing be postponed for several years are definitely out of order here. And so, of course, is any request that "just this once" the guest abandon principle for the sake of (someone else's) good time. What is in order is a vegetarian meal.

This does not mean that one plops a steaming heap of mixed veg on the table and says, "I'm sorry, folks, but this is all there is," finger pointing accusingly at cowering non-carnivore, "X is a *vegetarian.*" It means concocting a meal without meat (or in the case of strict vegetarians, without such meat by-products as eggs and cheese). The trick—and the fun—is doing it so no one notices.

First courses are easy. What could be nicer than a beautifully steamed artichoke served hot with hollandaise or (for hardliners) cold with a lemony vinaigrette? Very little, I suppose, but lots of things could be just as nice: mushrooms à la Grecque, broiled mushroom caps stuffed with a duxelles of their stems and some heavy cream, eggs à la Russe . . . yum.

For the main course, good ol' pasta (varieties made without eggs are available in specialty stores). Spinach noodles served with a quick sauce of red, ripe tomatoes lightly sautéed in olive oil with garlic and fresh basil meet the strictest test (and a mild grated Parmesan can be placed on the table for nonbelievers). Or a ridiculously delicious and simple dish of cheese-and-spinach-stuffed ravioli, over which one pours pine nuts and chopped walnuts that have been sautéed in lots of butter and mixed with goodly quantities of heavy cream. For this, a sharper Romano cheese is preferable.

After such pleasures, salad is a breeze. But since it's a party, the salad should be special. Snow peas and endive in a sherry vinaigrette, maybe, or chilled broccoli florets in oil and garlic, or asparagus and pimiento, or romaine wilted with freshly sautéed garlic croutons. . . .

For dessert, pears poached in a vanilla-flavored red wine syrup are easy and elegant, and if your vegetarian tolerates it, a big bowl of whipped cream is a nice bonus. And for such folk, pastries of all and any sort are swell.

At this point, when the coffee is being passed and the wineglasses lovingly drained, contentment reigns. And no one—not even your least favorite cousin from Columbus—will feel deprived in the slightest. Indeed, when everyone's gone home, you might even find yourself saying to your co-conspirator, "You know, we should do this more often."

Not, mind you, that feeding a gang of meat-eaters automatically guarantees happiness all round. I was reminded of this one night when my cooking was interrupted by someone asking, a little faintly, "Are you, er, *spitting* on that meat?"

What our house guest really wanted to say, I suspect, and what she doubtless would have said had she not been possessed of iron self-control, was, "Stop spitting on my steak, you Bozo." I can certainly imagine myself reacting that way. Here she was, invited to the country by people she was just getting to know, and she escapes from the kitchen's frenzied salad-assembling to the uncluttered cool of the back porch. Where she sees me spitting all over her dinner.

Unsettling is what you might call it, and there's surely something to be said for the civility that enabled her to register her horror so delicately. If the politeness didn't actually bring out the best in me, it at least suppressed the worst, and I stifled a temptation to tell her how colorfully we make our salad dressing (heh, heh). Instead, an honest question got an honest answer. "No," I said, "I'm spitting *under* it."

I thought this was a distinction of such stunning cruciality that it would immediately relax her, but she continued to look troubled. "And it's only water," I added. "Clean water."

"Oh," she said.

This did not exactly seem a ringing vote of confidence, so I attempted—inadequately, I fear—further reassurance: "From the well."

"Oh," she said again. And then, before I could babble out any more inanities, she adopted the tone Desi used to take with Lucy just before he blew up, "Why are you spitting *near* the steak?"

"Because," I explained, "the kids have stolen the goddamn water pistols again."

Also, though I didn't say so at the time, it's kind of fun to spit on the fire. And if you are (a) cooking anything trickier than hot dogs and (b) without a water pistol, it's necessary. Consider a steak. When the fire is good and ready—at its hottest, with the surface of each chunk of charcoal totally white—you put the steak on the grill. After a few minutes, its fat begins to liquefy and drip onto the coals. A bit longer (when, you should pardon the expression, the fat is in the fire) and flames begin to leap from the melted fat toward the steak. Some people, at this critical juncture, do nothing. Theirs is a touching faith in nature, and I have witnessed folks pulling it off successfully, but their faith seems to me misplaced. For often, the flames, not content with burning up the odd fat droplet, begin to consume the steak proper. Steak thus prepared cannot so much be said to have cooked as to have been set afire. And, usually, to taste as though it had been.

The preferred option (preferred, at any rate, by me and Smokey the Bear) involves the judicious application of water to the blazing fat. In small amounts, it doesn't appreciably lower the temperature of the coals, and it means the steak gets cooked by the charcoal and not by itself. Playing fireman is most efficiently and amusingly done with a water pistol, but in emergencies, a sip of water taken into the mouth and promptly expelled at the offending flames will do nicely. But not in front of the guests.

Beyond that, there aren't a whole lot of rules for home entertainment. People go to parties to have a good time; to stop them from enjoying themselves requires a positive effort; one really has to *work* at insulting a guest. Decent human beings, when served a flat soufflé, don't consider it an insult but an accident.

(In fact, if the cook has sufficient aplomb to rename the dish before serving, it doesn't even have to be a failed soufflé; it can instead be a perfectly successful and delicious Norwegian specialty rarely served beyond the fjords.) Insults come not from trying too hard but from trying not at all; guests should not, for instance, sit down to dinner and find their sleeves stuck to a gob of morning oatmeal. Beyond that, you're pretty much in clover. Any further nervousness can be quickly resolved by consulting Estragon's Five Easy Rules for Home Dining Entertainment:

1. Consider the guest list. Though it's by now impossible to keep everyone's ex-lovers straight, you should try to avoid fistfights. If you must ask George Steinbrenner, postpone Billy Martin until next week.

2. Even a simple first course makes what follows it seem more special.

3. The menu should be something you can manage without a nervous breakdown. People who don't want to see the cook eat in restaurants.

4. Flowers, even the buck-a-bunch kind from the subway shops, indicate that *you* think this is a special occasion.

5. So does emptying the catbox.

CHARCOAL-BROILED EGGPLANT

This is a slightly unusual way to deal with the annual eggplant glut, and to combine the cooking of vegetables and meat on days when even the thought of turning on the oven is insupportable. (The eggplant, by the way, doesn't drip into the fire at all.) It goes wonderfully with charcoal-broiled steaks (spat-upon or otherwise) and makes an unusual first course for a vegetarian feast.

1. For each two diners, stem and split lengthwise 1 small eggplant.

2. Score the surface of each half, sprinkle heavily with salt, and put face down on a rack to drain for about a half hour.

3. Wipe the salt off thoroughly, and rub the skins and flesh of the eggplant with olive (or, special treat, walnut) oil and oregano. Put the eggplant, skin side down, on a grill set high over the coals.

4. As soon as the skin shows even the faintest hint of charring, put another dollop of oil on the flesh and turn them over. In about 10 minutes, the eggplant should be creamlike on the inside, with a slighly crisped surface. Serve immediately, as the fruit will turn bitter if it burns.

Cuisine New Right

*W*e declared the quadrennial meeting of the Pop Sociology Faculty inside my head last week, and we thought Important Thoughts about the 1980 presidential election. What did it all mean, we asked. Eventually we worked our way through the Reston-like big-domers and got to the nub of the matter: But is it good for the food?

We are, I regret to report, a mind divided. We know this is the end of something—and we even think we know of what—but what is to take its place? Lots of pushing and shoving amid the brain cells trying to figure that one out. But various possibilities emerge.

First of all, no more *cuisine nouvelle*. And a good thing, too. Most overrated program since the Great Society (remember that?). I have nothing against federal largesse—I used to line up for my gov't surplus peanut butter, flour, corn meal, and (yecch) tinned beef back in the pre-food-stamp days when I was in graduate school—but *cuisine nouvelle* was a classic liberal scam. Francophile, overexpensive, brilliantly conceived but (more often than not) disastrously executed. Health food for rich people. Less is more.

"No, no," cry the voices of Real America, rising from the west to make Strom Thurmanoid chairman of the Senate Judiciary Committee. "*More* is more." They're right. "Less is more" is a notion taken seriously only by those who can afford the double chocolate mousse cake for dessert. And while the vanguard of the New Right might wish certain people (women, for instance, and blacks, Hispanics, gays, you and me) to be happy with the less that we are about to get, the dominant theme of their victorious campaign was of piggery unleashed. "More is more," they cried. "More for *me*."

But of what? One possibility is that we are in for a steak-and-potatoes renaissance. Le Cygne will empty, and lines will circle around the block outside of Gallagher's. Unfortunately, since the Moral Majority is extremely skeptical about worldly pleasures, all the steaks—though huge—will be well done. If you don't like dry meat, go back to where you came from. And none of those damn kiwi tarts for dessert, either. From now on it's apple pie. Served with the people's choice of either vanilla ice cream or Velveeta.

Maybe not. Maybe the reactionary tendency is more classic. Back to Escoffier, to Carême, fish-inside-fish, spun-sugar centerpieces, *croquembouches*, no respectable meal without the fish course. More servants will be required, of course, but the elimination of the minimum wage will help. Also "temporary" permission for employers to hire imported labor. The kind built low and squatty to the salamander.

Nonsense, nonsense. What with Mom home all day minding the 2.4 children and walking Spot, she'll have time to cook up an American storm. Home-baked bread, apple pandowdy. Mmmm, boy, doesn't that sound good? Of course with Mom not bringing home a paycheck, there'll be a lot more meat loaf and tuna-noodle casserole, but that's a small price to pay for making America great again. And if Dad has to work a double-shift to make ends meet, that's fine, too. Cooking dinner is woman's work. Kids are only supposed to see their father on the weekend anyway, when they can all drive 70 miles an hour to the football game.

On second thought. I will have another slice of that calf's liver with shallots and raspberry vinegar.

~~~~~~~~~

OLD-FASHIONED BAKED BEANS NOUVELLE

On the still other hand, it could be Hooverville. In which case, this slightly twisted version of stick-to-your ribs cheap food will come in handy, though it's so good that you don't really need to wait for the Depression to serve it.

Bring a pound of rinsed pea beans to the boil in about 6 qts. water to which you've added 3 or 4 peeled garlic cloves and a whole peeled onion. After about 10 or 15 minutes on the boil, cover the pot and place it in a warm oven.

After an hour or so, drain the beans, reserving the cooking liquid, and discard the onion and garlic. Line the bottom of a heavy ceramic casserole (or, if you're blessed with one, a bean crock) with 3 or 4 one-inch cubes of salt pork, another large onion, peeled and quartered, and several chunks of peeled, cored apple (or maybe a few grapes). Cover this with the beans.

Mix together, in some proportion that suits your fancy for sweet or sour, approximately ½ cup molasses-and-brown-sugar in a 50-50 ratio, ¼ to ½ cup cider vinegar, ¼ cup catsup, and a couple of tablespoons good prepared mustard. Add salt and pepper, and pour this glop into the beans. Stir once or twice, then pour in enough of the hot reserved bean liquid to cover (save any extra, the beans may need more as they cook).

Bake, covered, in a slow (300-degree) oven for about 6 hours; if you're rushed, you can do it in 4 hours by setting the temperature at 350—but no more.

Phyllistine

*I*t was about four-thirty in the afternoon, and thanks to a miracle of modern communications, I was able to sit in an office at *The Voice* and carry on a conversation with the Woman Warrior, who was standing in a Brooklyn kitchen at the time. The content of our conversation was admittedly on the mundane side—what would we have for dinner?—but our disagreement was spirited. The way I figure it, the invention of the telephone gave me an extra hour-and-a-half of brooding time, and I suppose I should be grateful. Otherwise, when the D train made its regular, though technically unscheduled, halt in the middle of the Manhattan Bridge, I might have frittered away those few minutes' delay lusting after Phyllis Schlafly instead of considering my domestic responsibilities.

Since these included dinner, I was able to sublimate sexual lust and focus on that nice spinach terrine in my shopping bag, but it was a continuing struggle. Ever since I saw her on television saying that virtuous women were never subject to sexual harassment, la belle Schlafly *sans merci* hath had me in thrall. God how she turns me on! Those eyes . . . those—dare I say it—ankles.

Anyway, it turns out that the Woman Warrior suffers more

from spring than I do. For about two weeks every year, she becomes utterly indifferent to cooking. Eating is okay, but the whole idea of shopping and washing and cutting and cooking and carving seems just too much. During those weeks, she would dine cheerfully on some nice runny cheese, a few pieces of sweet fruit, and a crusty loaf. Eaten, ideally, *al fresco.*

. . . There are no cooling breezes in the elevator. There is only the musky smell of Southern senators and anti-abortionists, a mingled scent as hotly erotic as hibiscus. Phyllis is in a pink suit, the ruffled collar of her pale-lilac blouse peeks over the pink, and between that colorful efflorescence and the disciplined knot of her hair, a tiny strip of still paler pink is exposed. This nape, this perfect part so private that even she has never looked upon it, is—perhaps from the heat, perhaps from some secret excitement at the testimony she is about to give—bedewed. Those inner essences, glistening, draw me forward. My tongue emerges and slowly, gratefully, bathes itself in them. She leans back. There is a rustle of silk, a creak of corsetry—

And a sudden jerk as the D train decides it wants to go to De Kalb Avenue after all. The telephone company, the Transit Authority, those twin symbols of corporate and governmental power strain mightily to frustrate my fantasies. What avails the firm round loaves of semolina bread, their unyielding surfaces hiding a velvet softness? What matters my earlier telephoned instruction to remove the butter from the refrigerator so that its unguent pliancy will be at a peak when I arrive. I am maddened with thoughts of Phyllis. Atlantic Avenue . . . Seventh Avenue . . . Prospect Park . . .

She is wearing stockings of course. My Phyllis would never dream of appearing in public with her limbs unsheathed. The shoes, buttery pink leather, have heels just high enough to flatter her lovely calves, just low enough to be sensible. Her legs, clad in petroleum by-product, are twin towers of virtue above them. On, Phyllis, I am ashamed even to mention them, afraid that you may—for even one moment—imagine yourself to be like other women. That you might think your fantasy-sullied virtue makes you the same as the scared teen-aged girl being groped on a commuter train by a man old enough to be her father, that you are just as much at risk as the painted hussies who opened their doors to the Boston Strangler.

But now that I think about it, there's not much danger that you will. I can go on, dreaming of that wonderful moment when at last I plunge—

Out of the tunnel, into the sun. There is a breeze now, and green trees flashing overhead to cool my reckless ardor. Composing myself, I leave the train at Newkirk Plaza and walk homeward. I stop to pick up catfood and milk. I will go home and kiss my wife, admire my daughter's belly button. We will put her to bed, and sip white wine while we eat our pâtés. I will try to be a kind and considerate husband. With God's help, I shall not mutter aloud in my dreams that forbidden name of . . . Phyllis.

SPRING SPAGHETTI

The search for the cookless dinner is considerably less strain than any of Erica Jong's quests, and the rewards more predictable. This uncooked spaghetti sauce is at its perfection when midsummer brings fresh basil and vine-ripe tomatoes onto the market, but it's possible to rush the season a little. Pierre Franey's collected *60-Minute Gourmet* has a couple of versions of this dish, but this recipe, which serves four generously, is adapted from *Alfredo Viazzi's Italian Cooking*.

1. Core and chop 8 medium tomatoes (you should get between 30 and 40 bitlets per tomato) and dump them into a glass or ceramic bowl along with ¾ cup good olive oil, 1 teaspoon wine vinegar, a handful of chopped parsley, 1 teaspoon dried basil (in summer, 6 leaves of fresh basil instead of the parsley-and-dried), salt and black pepper (or maybe some red pepper

flakes). Stir thoroughly, and let marinate at room temperature for 2 or 3 hours.

2. Cook 1 lb. vermicelli until just tender, drain and return it to the cooking pot. Pour the tomatoes and their marinade over it and serve at once with a little grated Parmesan on the side.

L'Envoi

Acornucopia

"**O**nce upon a time, not so long ago, there were two squirrels named Leander and Alexander who lived at the very top of an old sycamore tree in Flatbush. They were pretty much like all other squirrels—they climbed trees, jumping from branch to branch, and they chattered at the cats and people who walked below—except for one thing: they could talk.

"This was very handy for them, because instead of just running around in circles and dropping nuts on strangers the way other squirrels do when they get bored, Leander and Alexander could just sit quietly and have lovely conversations. One of their favorite things to talk about was food. Late in the afternoons, before they had their dinner and went to bed, they played a little game of listing all the wonderful things they'd like to eat.

"It was Alexander who first mentioned the acorn soufflé. Well 'soufflé' is such a silly sounding word that it made Leander giggle so much he almost fell out of the tree. Alexander knew when he had a good thing going, so for many weeks he embroidered and embellished the idea of the perfect acorn soufflé. It was, he said, served at Lutèce, and someday they would go there and order it. Putting on a transparently phony French accent, he pretended to be Monsieur Soltner himself, 'Ah, M'sieu Squir*ell*,' he said, bowing in front of Leander, 'we have for you today zee treat especial, zee *délicat* soufflé des acorns. *C'est très, très délicieux.*' And Leander, of course, giggled some more.

"Eventually, they had talked so much about this adventure that it became almost real to them, and one day Leander said, 'Let's *do* it.'

" 'Do what?'

" 'Go to Lutèce and get an acorn soufflé.'

" 'I don't know if that's really a good idea, Leander. They might not let us in, you know. It's a very fancy place. Besides, it's all the way in Manhattan. How would we get there?'

" 'Easy,' said Leander, 'we take the train. You've seen all those people getting on it in the morning. That's what they're doing, going in to have lunch at Lutèce.'

" 'Really?' asked Alexander, who was beginning to get interested in the idea despite his better judgment. But then he said, 'We couldn't. We don't have any tokens.'

" 'Silly,' said Leander. 'We don't need tokens. The train runs above ground here, and the cars pass right under our tree. When one slows down, the way they sometimes do, we could just drop down on top of a car.'

"Which they did. Unfortunately, since they'd never taken the train before, they were a little confused, and they got on the train that was going *away* from the city. So instead of winding up near Lutèce, they found themselves all the way out in Coney Island.

" 'Are you sure this is the place, Leander?' asked Alexander. They were passing by a throw-the-baseball-and-knock-over-the-cats game. 'This doesn't look like a neighborhood where you get a lot of fancy restaurants.'

" 'Of course it is,' said Leander bravely, though he was beginning to have some doubts himself. 'I'll just ask someone for directions,' and he went up to the man who ran the baseball-tossing booth. 'Excuse me, sir,' he said, 'can you tell us the way to Lutèce?'

"The man, whose name was Tony Speraducci, looked down at

him. 'You gotta be kidding,' he said. 'You're a squirrel. Only way you're ever gonna get into Lutèce is if Soltner adds Brunswick Stew to the menu.'

"This was, when you think about it, a pretty insensitive remark, and Leander burst into tears. He was blubbering away about acorn soufflés when Tony interrupted him. 'Listen, kid, I'm sorry I hurt your feelings. Why don't you dry your eyes and stay for lunch with Marie and me. She runs the fortune-telling tent down there, and she cooks a mean frittata.'

" 'That would be very nice indeed,' said Leander, and he scampered back to tell Alexander about the invitation. Over the frittata—and it turns out Tony had not exaggerated Marie's skills—they began to talk about the carnival biz. Marie told them how she was able to foresee the future by sizing people up and figuring out what they wanted to hear, and Tony talked about how his cats were weighted so they were almost impossible to knock off. It was then that Alexander came up with the idea that he and Leander could help Marie. 'Listen,' he said, 'we could just hang out in front of your booth—who notices squirrels?—and listen to what people are saying before they come in. Then we'll sneak inside and tell you. With your ability and our knowledge, you'll be rolling in acorns.'

"And so she was. Within a few months, Marie had become the most famous fortune-teller in all New York. People lined up for hours outside her tent, and none of them paid any attention at all to the squirrels who were listening while they talked. Eventually, Marie was named Fortune-Teller of the Year by *People* magazine, and she and Tony were invited to a luncheon in her honor at Lutèce.

"It was a very wonderful lunch, and no one even noticed that Marie put half her acorn soufflé—a bite at a time—into her purse, and that Tony seemed to be feeding his into the side pocket of his jacket."

Now there comes about a five-minute interval, and the next voice is the Woman Warrior's: "Were you telling her a story?"

"Yes."

"I thought so. Only you would tell an eight-month-old baby a bedtime story about a soufflé."

"It worked, didn't it? She's asleep."

BAKED ACORN SQUASH

Other than in fantasy, I'm afraid there is no season for acorn soufflé, but winter squash—butternut, hubbard, acorn—is now coming onto the market in quantity. Here is a basic recipe for the small, acorn-shaped, green-and-yellow variety, together with a couple of variations.

1. Preheat oven to 400 degrees, and put a kettle of water on to boil. Split each squash in half lengthwise (1 squash serves 2), and scoop out the seeds.

2. When the water is boiling, pour it into a high-sided baking pan to a depth of about a half-inch. Put the squash, cut side down, into the pan and bake for a half hour.

3. Turn the squash halves over, and in the hollow of each put a scant tablespoon of salted butter and a couple of tablespoons of brown sugar. Continue baking until tender (another 10 or 15 minutes).

Variations: maple syrup instead of brown sugar, a dollop of dry sherry along with the sugar, a grating of nutmeg and a tablespoon of fresh parsley (and maybe a little extra butter), in place of the sugar. All good.

Index